The Jesus Cult:

2000 Years of the Last Days

By
Robert Conner

Table of Contents

DEDICATION i

ACKNOWLEDGEMENT ii

ABOUT THE AUTHOR iii

FOREWORD iv

Part 1: CHRISTIAN CULTS 1

Part 2: THE LAST DAYS 7

Part 3: THE RISING SON? 26

Part 4: JESUS FAMILY VALUES 52

Part 5: FACT EXEMPT, TAX EXEMPT, ABOVE THE

LAW 67

Part 6: THE SKEPTIC'S *PANARION* 94

REFERENCES 107

DEDICATION

Hector Avalos, in memoriam.

ACKNOWLEDGEMENT

I must first acknowledge editor/publisher Mogg Morgan for his early support and expertise, Edwin Suominen at Tellectual Press, and Isaac Levine and the team at Amazon.

I am also deeply indebted to John Loftus at the *Debunking Christianity* blog and to David Madison for their friendship and encouragement.

ABOUT THE AUTHOR

Robert Conner studied biblical languages and read biblical criticism at Western Kentucky University from 1975 until 1977. He deconverted a few years later, but retained his interest in Christian origins. He began a writing career in 1983, and in 2006 published *Jesus the Sorcerer: Exorcist and Prophet of the Apocalypse*, a survey of magical praxis in the New Testament. Several other books on the same subject followed.

In 2015 Conner expanded a previously written essay into a book about the Secret Gospel of Mark controversy, and in 2018 , intrigued by the similarities between the post-mortem appearances of Jesus in the gospels of Luke and John and Greco-Roman ghost lore, published *Apparitions of Jesus: The Resurrection as Ghost Story. The Jesus Cult* is Conner's tenth book.

Contact: thejesuscult58@gmail.com

FOREWORD

John W. Loftus, MDiv, MTh

Citing plenty of Roman writers familiar with the early Jesus Cult, along with teasing out the true meaning from New Testament sources, Robert Conner makes a solid case that "Christianity was a cult from its inception, a toxic brew of apocalyptic delusion, sexual phobias and fixations, with a hierarchy of control, control of women by men, of slaves by masters, and of society by the church." It had an "irrational and antisocial nature" to it, and "its destructive features remain a clear and present danger today. Its greatest threat is the core feature of the Christian cult: belief in belief, the conviction that the Christian narrative is literally its own proof."

To say I agree with Conner is a huge understatement. I love how he writes! Readers will find a great amount of erudition combined with an unmatched use of rhetoric and even hilarity in his book. I am honored and delighted to write this Foreword for another excellent book by him.

Conner says Christianity was never anything more than a cult "in the most pejorative sense of the word." In the chapters to follow, he makes his case and shows that religious cults share with Christianity "several familiar features" like "a fixation on sexual purity, bizarre interpretations of scripture, and often a preoccupation with

End Times theology which leads members to interpret events through an apocalyptic lens."

Paul's Christianity.

Religious cults "have charismatic leaders, living or dead, who have all the answers" and/or direct communication from a god, goddess, angels, demons, or other divine beings of some kind. When it comes to the Christian faith, the apostle Paul was that charismatic person. In the Gospels, Jesus is presented as the original charismatic leader, a prophet like Moses, the long-awaited Messiah, the son of God, co-creator of the universe, and divine redeemer of all flesh, who is supposed to return to reign on high forever, being joined to the hip—as it were—to the second person of the trinity.

It's doubtful whether such a Jesus character existed as a person in the past.[1] But even if Jesus' character was indeed a conglomerate mix of several real personages found in the Gospels, it would be false to say he was the founder of Christianity. New Testament scholar Gerd Lüdemann shows this decisively in his book, *Paul: The Founder of Christianity* (Prometheus Books, 2002).

Lüdemann comes to the conclusion that Paul should be considered not only Christianity's most influential proselytizer but, in truth, deserves the title of founder of the religion that ostensibly originated with Jesus of Nazareth. Though other scholars have previously made the point that Paul's interpretation of the Christian message actually obscured the original teachings of Jesus, Lüdemann goes further. His painstaking historical research shows that Paul created the major tenets of the Christianity we know today and that his theology—an original synthesis of Hebrew and Greek belief systems—differs significantly from what we now know the historical Jesus to have preached.[2]

Conner previously argued that Paul, the founder of Christianity, was basically crazy.[3] After marshaling the evidence, some of which I'll rehearse below, he concluded: "Modern psychology with superior investigative techniques and tools can now question whether Paul of Tarsus was functionally, if not clinically, insane—and whether the religion he championed is based on delusion."[4]

For my part, I can affirm with a great deal of confidence that Paul was functionally insane *if he were living among rational people*. But in a rational society, Paul wouldn't function well at all. He would be that homeless guy on the street corner who proselytized with a bullhorn and a sign, "REPENT! FOR THE END IS NEAR!" But since there were like-minded superstitious people in the ancient Roman world, Paul seemed to function fairly well. After all, he gained a following by convincing enough people to believe what he said, and he was financially taken care of by his flock while being persecuted. Whether someone is a functioning person has much to do with the kind of world, society, or tribe one resides in. Paul was able to function in the ancient Roman world because that world, as described by historian and philosopher Richard Carrier, was an age of *Kooks and Quacks*.[5]

However, I think Paul might be diagnosed as clinically insane in a real sense. Let's go with this definition from Law.com: "Insanity: mental illness of such a severe nature that a person cannot distinguish fantasy from reality, cannot conduct her/his affairs due to psychosis, or is subject to uncontrollable impulsive behavior."[6] Try this definition of *psychosis* from an authoritative mental health website from England:

Psychosis is when people lose some contact with reality. The two main symptoms of psychosis are:

—*hallucinations* – where a person hears, sees, and, in some cases, feels, smells, or tastes things that do not exist outside their mind but can feel very real to the person affected by them; a common hallucination is hearing voices

—*delusions* – where a person has strong beliefs that are not shared by others; a common delusion is someone believing there's a conspiracy to harm them.[7]

This sounds about right to me. Paul was clinically insane in some real sense, just not necessarily functionally insane in the world he lived in.

Hearing and heeding imaginary voices in one's head as if they came from a god, angel, or spirit *is not the mark of a sane person*, particularly if the voices command things that are harmful and dangerous, deceptive and false, and they control much of a person's life. That's what we see throughout the Bible, in both the Old and New Testaments. In the Old Testament, we often read how "The word of the Lord came to me." Take seriously what you read of Abraham, Elijah, Moses, Jeremiah, Ezekiel, Zechariah, Jonah, Joel, Hosea, Obadiah, and some others. Just imagine the story of Abraham, who is told to sacrifice his son Isaac. He was really going to kill his son! Three major monotheistic religions heap high praise on him for going ahead with it. That's insane! Every court of a sane country based on the law would agree. The only sane defense would be insanity.

There are plenty of others. Think of what the gospel according to Matthew says of Joseph, the alleged father of Jesus. He was convinced by a dream that Mary, who was believed by him to be a virgin, was pregnant as the result of divine impregnation. (Matthew 1:19-24) Yes, a dream! At this point, believers are faced with a fatal dilemma to their faith. If this is the kind of "evidence" that went into writing the gospels, we shouldn't believe anything else they say without corroborating objective evidence. But if providing evidence was unnecessary for writing their gospels—because they were divinely inspired—why do gospel writers give us the pretense of having researched into it (see Luke 1:1–4)? Why not simply say their stories are true due to divine inspiration and be done with the pretense? Of course, then the gig would be up, the sham uncovered.

Paul and the Corinthian believers were visionaries based on the prophecy of Joel 2:28, quoted in Acts 2:17: "Your sons and daughters will see visions, your old men will dream dreams." They were convinced they were receiving divine messages from Jesus and expressed these revelations in church worship through the "spiritual gifts" of divine "wisdom," "knowledge," "prophecy," or "tongues" (1 Cor. 12:7–10). Acts describes several of Paul's visions (Acts 16:9–10; 18:9; 22:17–18; 23:11) that showed him where to travel next, who to talk to, and what to say. In Galatians 2:1-2, his god told him to go meet "privately" with esteemed leaders of the church in Jerusalem. Would a god really micromanage Paul's life like that? Only deranged people, clinically insane people in a real sense, believe that an almighty creator and ruler of the universe pays specific attention to the details of their travels.

Paul repeatedly speaks of "revelations" that he passed down to the church (1 Cor. 2:13; 7:40; 14:37). He even says he learned the details of the Lord's Supper the night Jesus was betrayed from "the Lord" himself (1 Cor. 11:23). Rationalist philosopher G. A. Wells comments, "According, then, to Paul, the risen Jesus personally told him that he, Jesus, had, during his earthly life, instituted the Eucharist in this way." Wells go on to state the obvious: "One can easily envisage how all manner of rulings and doctrines could have emerged on such a basis, and in time be ascribed not to the risen Jesus but to the earthly Jesus."[8] And this is what we find. The apostle Peter reports he was in a *trance* (Acts 10:10; 11:5-7) [9] when he saw a vision imparting a major change of theology, which allowed for the Gentiles to be acceptable to their new religion without being circumcised.

Conner adds, "what makes Paul's private revelations from Jesus any more trustworthy than the revelations given Zarathushtra by Vohu Manah, or Muhammad's revelations from the angel Gabriel, or Moroni's private revelations to Joseph Smith, or for that matter the "mahatma" Koot Hoomi's disclosures of divine secrets to Helena Blavatsky. After all, by the time of Paul, spirits had been whispering secrets to mediums for millennia as evidenced by the Old Testament tale of Saul and the medium of En Dor." (1 Samuel 28:1-20).

Religious cults make these types of claims all the time. Braco "the Gazer" is believed to heal people by simply gazing into their eyes. Do you believe these things just because they say so? Of course, you don't. When it comes to religious sects, you were *not* indoctrinated to believe; you demand sufficient evidence before belief. But when it comes to the religious sect you were indoctrinated to believe, you don't demand any proof at all because you were likely taught to believe at the age of four years old—along with other imaginary beings like Santa Claus, Easter Bunny, and the Tooth Fairy. The threat of hell as a punishment in the afterlife reinforced your early childhood indoctrinated faith by searing it into your mind. The effect is like cattle rustlers using the technique of branding their cows. Once belief is seared into the child's mind, the child will be deathly afraid of questioning that indoctrination.

In the last book of the Bible, one that wasn't accepted very early into the canon of the New Testament, the author claimed to write his whole book based on a revelation by Jesus (Revelation 1:1-2). Revelation includes seven divinely dictated letters to seven early churches, chapters 2–3. Anyone could claim such things. Why should we believe anyone who makes these kinds of unevidenced unsubstantiated extraordinary claims? If Jesus is so smart, why didn't he write his own book?

If Paul and others writing the Old and New Testaments should not be taken seriously due to being clinically insane in some real sense, so also everyone who believes the Bible's words are "god-breathed" words could be considered insane in the same way.[10]

Belief in Belief Itself

This leads me to the issue of "belief in belief" which Conner correctly says is "the core feature of the Christian cult" and "the most alarming part about Christianity." Belief in belief itself "is the conviction that the Christian narrative is literally its own proof" by one's own personal subjective feelings when reading it devotionally. But in the last few decades, psychopathology has discovered overwhelming conclusive evidence "that *radical disconfirmation often has little effect on cult members*; some may be peeled away be dramatically failed predictions, revelations of financial fraud, or blatant moral hypocrisy, but even irrefutable evidence of criminality will often cause true believers to simply dig in."

Michael Shermer highlights this fact about belief in belief:

Most of us, most of the time come to our beliefs for a variety of reasons having little to do with empirical evidence and logical reasoning...Rather, such variables as genetic predispositions, parental predilections, sibling influences, peer pressures, educational experiences, and life impressions all shape the personality, preferences, and emotional inclinations that, in conjunction with numerous social and cultural influences, lead us to make certain belief choices. Rarely do any of us sit down before a table of facts, weigh them pro and con, and choose the most logical and rational belief, regardless of what we previously believed. Instead, the facts of the world come to us through the colored filters of the theories, hypotheses, hunches, biases, and prejudices we have accumulated through our lifetime. We then sort through the body of data and select those most confirming what we already believe and ignore or rationalize away those that are disconfirming.[11]

This malaise in human beings is hard-wired into our brains. Psychologist Gregory W. Lester explains:

Because senses and beliefs are both tools for survival and have evolved to augment one another, our brain considers them to be separate but equally important purveyors of survival information...This means that beliefs are designed to operate independent of sensory data. *In fact, the whole survival value of beliefs is based on their ability to persist in the face of contradictory evidence.* Beliefs are not supposed to change easily or simply in response to disconfirming evidence. If they did, they would be virtually useless as tools for survival...Skeptical thinkers must realize that because of the survival value of beliefs, disconfirming evidence will rarely, if ever, be sufficient to change beliefs, even in "otherwise intelligent" people...[S]keptics must always appreciate how hard it is for people to have their beliefs challenged. It is, quite literally, a threat to their brain's sense of survival. It is entirely normal for people to be defensive in such situations. The brain feels it is fighting for its life...it should be comforting to all skeptics to remember that the truly amazing part of all of this is not that so few beliefs change or that people can be so irrational, but that anyone's beliefs ever change at all. Skeptics' ability to alter their own beliefs in response to data is a true gift, a unique, powerful, and precious ability. It is genuinely a "higher brain function" in that it goes against some of the most natural and fundamental biological urges.[12]

Guy P. Harrison put it this way. If a skeptic disputes a psychic's readings, then "the believer's brain is likely to instinctively go into siege mode. The drawbridge is raised, crocodiles are released into the moat, and defenders man the walls…The worst part of all this is that the believer usually doesn't recognize how biased and close-minded he is being. He likely feels that he is completely rational and fair. It doesn't happen just with fans of psychics. We are all vulnerable to this distorted way of thinking."[13]

This process is triggered whenever the brain feels threatened by contrary data, and it's not just the religious beliefs we're talking about. The brain feels physically attacked when confronted with ideas that challenge it and will do what it takes to deflect that attack. Dr. Jonas Kaplan, an assistant research professor of psychology at the University of Southern California, and his research team studied the brain scans of people while being challenged about their *political* beliefs. The study uncovered a correlation: When a belief is directly challenged by new information, the brain kicks into a defensive mode ***exactly as if it was being physically threatened***. Kaplan: "The brain can be thought of as a very sophisticated self-defense machine. If there is a belief that the brain considers part of who we are, it turns on its self-defense mode to protect that belief."[14]

The job of the evolved human brain is not primarily to get at the truth. Its primary job is to protect us from harm by keeping us in a socially acceptable caring tribal grouping with whom we feel support and can turn to for help in times of need. This means the brain makes us conform to one's own tribe. Nonconformists could be kicked out of the tribe, and that was dangerous. That being acknowledged, we know the two-step solution!

The first step is to acknowledge this problem as a very serious one. Compare it to Alcoholics Anonymous, whose first step is to admit they are alcoholics. The problem is the evolved brain won't allow us to seriously entertain facts that disrupt our personal, social and tribal comfort zone. It will do everything it can to reject them.

The second step is to resolve to disarm the brain's defensive mechanism, to demand sufficient evidence, objective evidence, and scientific evidence, if possible, for what we will accept as true about the world we live in, its nature, its workings and its origins. Not dogma reinforced by any creed or nationalism.

The indoctrinated brain comes up with all kinds of excuses not to see logic: non-sequiturs, special pleadings, red-herrings, and double standards.[15] I must question what I believe as well, but there is a difference that makes all the difference. I know what does not count as sufficient evidence for the miracle claims in the Bible. Second- third- fourth-hand hearsay doesn't count, nor does circumstantial evidence, nor anecdotal evidence as reported in documents that are centuries later than the supposed events, documents copied by scribes and theologians who had no qualms about including forgeries. I also know that subjective feelings or experiences or inner voices don't count as extraordinary evidence, nor someone who tells others his writings are inspired, nor divine communication through dreams, or visions. If we can agree with this, we agree on a lot. Sadly, many believers don't care if their belief meets any standards of evidence. They believe what comforts them regardless of whether it's true or not.

I call it the outsider test for faith (OTF). You should examine religious claims as an outsider—a nonbeliever—as much as possible, applying the same objective standards to your own religious sect as you do to the many other religious sects you reject. If you're a Christian, treat your faith as if you're non-Christian, and if you're a Muslim, treat your faith as if you're a non-Muslim, and so forth. Hypothetically become a nonbeliever. See what it looks like to someone who does not believe in it at all. Treat them all as an agnostic would, which I call this default position. For if it doesn't convince nonbelievers, it won't convince anyone else either.

Rene Descartes, considered the father of modern philosophy, said: "If you would be a real seeker after truth, it is necessary that at least once in your life, you doubt, as far as possible, all things." This should be a rite of passage into adulthood. Philosopher Stephen Law explains what we must overcome to get at the truth: "Anything based on faith, no matter how ludicrous, can be made to be consistent with the available evidence, given a little patience and ingenuity."[16] Theists have had about 2000 years to do this. Anthropologist James Houk agrees that "virtually anything and everything, no matter how absurd, inane, or ridiculous, has been believed or claimed to be true at one time or another by somebody, somewhere in the name of faith."[17] I'm arguing along with atheist author George Smith that "faith as an alleged method of acquiring knowledge is totally invalid."[18] It's not just your religious dogmas that are unreasonable. It's how you arrive at and maintain them. As Peter Boghossian has argued, "Belief in god is not the problem. Belief without evidence is the problem. Warrantless, dogged confidence is the problem." He adds, "The most charitable thing we can say about faith is that it's likely to be false."[19]

Belief in belief has no method for acquiring objective knowledge. Faith is folly. Reasonable people should all think exclusively in terms of the probabilities by "proportioning their conclusions according to the strength of the evidence," as philosopher *par excellence* David Hume said. When you do that, you'll see why religious faith is unreasonable. The goal of the OTF is to help eliminate cognitive biases so people of faith can clearly and honestly evaluate his or her religion. It's that simple.

The outsider test is designed to help believers see the need for requiring sufficient objective evidence. Believers can play lip service to this requirement by saying they accept it. But what is meant isn't always readily apparent. The test also helps them see what is meant by sufficient objective evidence. That's it. In other words, the outsider test helps believers twice-over. ***It's both a test and a teaching tool.*** The test helps believers to accept the requirement for sufficient objective evidence (all by itself a hard task!). But it goes on to teach believers what it means by forcing them to consider how they reasonably examine the other religious faiths they reject. It teaches them to apply the same single standard across the board to their own religious faith.

John W. Loftus

June, 2022

Part 1: CHRISTIAN CULTS

"Drinking the Kool-Aid" entered the American lexicon after 918 followers of faith healer Jim Jones, leader of the People's Temple, committed murder-suicide *en masse* in 1978. In 1993, the Branch Davidians, led by David Koresh, their self-proclaimed "final prophet," engaged in a prolonged siege and gun battle with US federal agents that left 75 people dead, 25 of them children. Today the sect, an offshoot of the Seventh-Day Adventists, has reorganized as The Branch, The Lord Our Righteousness. Mormons, Jehovah's Witnesses, the Unification Church, Christian Identity, Pentecostalism, the Westboro Baptist Church, the Church of Scientology, and Christian Science, are often labeled as cults due to a defining characteristic: charismatic leaders, living or dead, who have all the answers.

Religious cults have several familiar features besides claims of divine revelation given to larger-than-life figures—a fixation on sexual purity, bizarre interpretations of scripture, and often a preoccupation with End Times theology which leads members to interpret events through an apocalyptic lens. Most alarming, however, is evidence of psychopathology among religious believers, a feature that has only recently been the subject of serious investigation. Most would probably agree that "it is the way in which psychosis and spirituality have been kept so distinct that demands explanation."[20]

1

Experience has shown that radical disconfirmation often has little effect on cult members; some may be peeled away by dramatically failed predictions, revelations of financial fraud, or blatant moral hypocrisy, but even irrefutable evidence of criminality will often cause true believers to simply dig in. Although several egregious examples will be mentioned, this book is not a catalog of the horrors of religious cults—news of fraud, child abuse and neglect, and serial sexual predation in Christian churches makes the headlines on a weekly basis. Neither is this book primarily a refutation of Christian theological assertions. Instead, this work defends the claim that Christianity was a cult as presently understood from its inception, a toxic brew of apocalyptic delusion, sexual phobias and fixations, and a hierarchy of control, control of women by men, of slaves by masters, and society by the church. Christianity's irrational and antisocial nature was fully documented by Roman writers familiar with the early Jesus Cult, and its destructive features, intrinsic to "biblical Christianity," remain a clear and present danger. However, the greatest threat is the core feature of the Christian cult: *belief in belief*, the conviction that the Christian narrative is literally its own proof.

Today the field of New Testament studies is more contentious than ever. After decades of debate about how much—if any—of the gospel stories is based on real events, even the existence of Jesus of Nazareth has been credibly called into question.[21] Tens of thousands of books, articles,

2

and blogs have been published that purport to explain the New Testament; by some estimates, more than 5000 books on Christianity are released annually in the United States alone. Besides this avalanche of publications, there are currently over 20 peer-reviewed journals of religion in English as well, most published quarterly, several of which focus exclusively on early Christianity. In short, it is safe to say that the 27 books of the New Testament are the most thoroughly debated set of documents in world history, subjected interminably, generation after generation, to word-by-word analysis, all without the emergence of a consensus of opinion regarding the accuracy, the historicity, the intention, or in some cases even the meaning of nearly any of it.

Historians have treated Christianity with extreme deference. "A combination of theological, cultural, and historical factors has conspired to create a protected enclave for this particular religion. As a consequence, methods and techniques that are taken for granted in the treatment of other religions have been ignored or discarded in dealing with this one…the further assumption has been made, with however much sophistication, that certain events in early Christianity are not only historically distinctive but in some sense religiously unique."[22] As one historian remarked, "dogmatic images of normative Christian origins are not only reinforced every Sunday during worship but are also subconsciously lodged in the minds of scholars."[23]

The text of the New Testament contains around 184,600 words with some 300,000 to 400,000 variant readings depending on which Greek master text scholars consider most authentic based on debatable criteria—by way of comparison, the fantasy novel *Harry Potter and the Goblet of Fire* contains 190,637 words. After centuries of study and debate, "authorities" on the New Testament are divided about what the first Christians believed and when they believed it, if the "original text" of the gospels and letters of Paul can be recovered, if the text is meant to be read literally or allegorically, where the mostly anonymous writers got their vocabulary and ideas, what terms like "faith" really mean, and whether some (or any) of the events related in the gospels and Acts really happened (or not). Recently other, more basic, questions have been credibly raised: did Jesus himself exist? Were his followers visionaries or just garden-variety lunatics?

It is widely recognized that the only New Testament text from the second century is P52, a papyrus fragment about the size of a credit card that preserves a bit of text from the gospel of John. Given that more than a century passed between the original documents—the autographs—and the first surviving copies of the New Testament books, the evidence for Jesus and his first disciples is based entirely, *one hundred percent*, on writings of questionable historicity and that the writings that survived were subject to revision in the process of being copied, are there really any

4

authorities on primitive Christianity or is all of it ultimately just guesswork, pure speculation?

Citing "the original Greek" of the New Testament texts presupposes the recovery of the original text is even attainable. Eldon Epp, a noted textual critic writing in a seminal article, identifies four stages of the text, a "predecessor text-form," an "autographic text-form," the text as it "left the desk" of the writer, a "canonical text-form" that "became normative for faith and practice," and an "interpretive text-form, representing any and each interpretive iteration or reformulation of a writing—as it was used in the life, worship, and teaching of the church—or of individual variants so created and used." Epp concluded, "reality and maturity require that textual criticism face unsettling facts, chief among them that the term 'original' has exploded into a complex and highly unmanageable multivalent entity. Whatever tidy boundaries textual criticism may have presumed in the past have now been shattered…"[24] In short, the text was fluid before it became stable, and copyists were not copying machines but members of communities with varying interpretations of scripture who were willing and able to make the text reflect their beliefs as they reproduced it. Even scholars who remain true believers admit "the N[ew] T[estament] that we now have is to a great extent OUR modern construct (it was never used by anyone in the early church)."[25] It is also worth remembering that

Jesus' primary, *and likely only language*, was Aramaic, not Greek.

There is evidently a growing realization among legions of clergy persons laboring in hundreds of denominations that religion is little more than a sop offered to the justifiably fearful and confused, and that the antics of religious shills, grifters, frauds, reactionaries, and crazies are driving rational people away from churches in droves. In light of the kingdom of darkness proposed by Christian theocrats, it can fairly be asked if Christianity was ever more than a cult in the most pejorative sense of the word.

Part 2: THE LAST DAYS

The first mention of Jesus that has survived until the present is found in the writings of Paul of Tarsus. Although Paul was traditionally credited with writing fourteen of the twenty-seven books of the New Testament, the majority of modern New Testament specialists consider the authorship of only five to be beyond dispute—1 Thessalonians, Romans, Galatians, Philemon, and Philippians—but most also accept, with certain caveats, that 1 and 2 Corinthians were written by Paul as well. In any case, to discover what at least some of the first Christians believed, we must begin with Paul, who probably wrote his letters between 50 to 60 C.E.

Few passages from Paul's letters reflect the intensity of his End Times convictions more clearly than his advice on sex and marriage: "It is good for a man not to have sexual relations with a woman…I mean, brothers, is that the time is short. From now on, those who have wives should live as if they do not…For this world in its present form is passing away." (1 Corinthians 7:1, 29, 31) Even though Paul makes concessions for those who lack self-control, his clear preference is a Christian "household of brothers and sisters rather than husbands and wives, fathers and mothers."[26] The return of Christ is so close that even married couples are to act as if celibate.

A sense of urgency pervades Paul's letters: "Do this, understanding the allotted time: the hour has already arrived for you to awaken from sleep, for now our salvation is nearer than when we first believed...the night is nearly spent, the day is about to break." (Romans 13:11-12) "...as you eagerly await our Lord Jesus Christ to be revealed...judge nothing before the appointed time; wait until the Lord comes...These things happened to them as examples and were written down as warnings for us, on whom the culmination of the ages has come." (1 Corinthians 1:7, 4:5, 10:11)

Paul composes his apocalyptic *pièce de résistance*, his earliest letter, in response to the unexpected death of some in the house church of the Thessalonians. The Second Coming is mentioned frequently. (1 Thessalonians 1:10, 2:19-20, 3:13, 4:13-18, 5:1-11, 23-24) After praising his converts' "deep conviction," Paul reminds them of "how you turned to God from idols to serve the living and true God and to wait for his Son from heaven" and asks, "For what is our hope, our joy, or the crown in which we will glory in the presence of the Lord Jesus when he comes? Is it not you?" Paul prays "that you will be blameless and holy in the presence of our God and Father when our Lord Jesus comes with all his holy ones." (1 Thessalonians 1:4, 9-10, 2:19, 3:13) Finally, Paul comes to the crux of his letter, the unexpected death of believers: "Brothers, we do not want you to be uninformed about those who sleep in death, so that you do not grieve like the rest of mankind who have no hope.

For we believe Jesus died and rose again, and we believe God will bring with Jesus those who have fallen asleep in him. According to the Lord's word, we tell you that we who are still alive, who are left until the coming of the Lord, will certainly not precede those who have fallen asleep. For the Lord himself will come down from heaven with a loud command, with the voice of the archangel and with the trumpet call of God, and the dead in Christ will rise first. After that, we who are still alive and are left will be caught up together with them in the clouds to meet the Lord in the air. And so we will be with the Lord forever." (1 Thessalonians 4:14-17)

Paul clearly believed most of his converts would live to see the return of Jesus—"we the living who survive" makes no sense unless those who received his letter, "the church of the Thessalonians," expected to be physically present to witness the Second Coming. Paul's wish, "may your whole spirit and soul and *body be preserved blameless until our Lord Jesus comes back*" (1 Thessalonians 1:1, 5:23), clearly presupposes the members of his church would still be bodily, corporeally, alive when "Jesus comes back." "We the living who survive" as well as "*we will not all sleep*, but we will all be changed" (1 Corinthians 15:51) were addressed in letters to *living people who did not expect to die*. "Paul taught his converts that the Lord would return so soon that they would live to see the day…Death was not expected."[27] "The appearance of Christ is ardently awaited as the fulfillment of their hope, as the attainment of salvation and as the crowning of Paul's preaching the word of God to them...The expectation is that Paul, and others, will live to see the Lord's coming."[28]

The death of early believers was clearly an unexpected crisis that required reassurance about the imminent return of the Lord: "we will glory...when our Lord comes...you will be blameless and holy...when our Lord comes...may your...body be kept blameless at the coming of our Lord...(2:20, 3:13, 5:23) Preaching the imminent end of the existing age is the bedrock of primitive Christian belief, a fact widely acknowledged in mainstream New Testament studies: "the Second Coming of Jesus will occur in the immediate future...the vast majority of Christians would be living witnesses to Christ's return from heaven."[29] Paul's teaching "is uncharacteristically clear and consistent throughout his letters. Believers, whether living or dead, will receive a new, glorious body, like Christ's at his resurrection—and this will happen very, very soon... Paul and his communities are troubled by the death of believers before Christ's Second Coming: they did not expect this and don't know what to make of it."[30] "The earliest Christians were Jews who believed that they were living at the end of the age and that Jesus himself was to return from heaven as a cosmic judge of the earth."[31]

Obviously, Jesus didn't "come down from heaven with a loud command, with the voice of an archangel and with the

10

trumpet call of God," and none of the Thessalonians were "caught up with [the resurrected dead] in the clouds to meet the Lord in the air." The first generation of Christians missed the Second Coming bus, as would every generation to follow, and we know that fact caused some comment: "…you must understand that in the last days scoffers will come, scoffing and following their own evil desires. They will say, 'Where is this "coming" he promised? Ever since our ancestors died, everything goes on as it has since the beginning of creation.'" (2 Peter 3:3-4) The author, writing at the end of the first century, is still convinced Christians are living in "the last days" but concedes that the Christian ancestors have died and "everything goes on as it has since the beginning of creation." Paul's predictions failed. The blameless dead, sexually unblemished, are all still in the ground. The hollow promises of the Christian prophets in Paul's churches were false and would be disproved again and again, generation after generation, century after century.

Paul never met the Jesus of the gospels. In point of fact, Paul shows no particular interest in or familiarity with the career of Jesus. His letters have almost nothing in common with the gospel stories—Paul never mentions the virgin birth, Jesus' infancy, the miracles, or the transfiguration, and barely alludes to Jesus' teaching. For Paul, Jesus only gets interesting after he's dead: "I determined not to know anything while I was among you except Jesus Christ and him crucified." (1 Corinthians 2:2) Although he is the first to

11

declare Jesus is the son of God, Paul connects Jesus' sonship not with his birth (Luke 1:35) or with his baptism (Mark 1:11), but with his resurrection: "[Jesus] was constituted the Son of God in power through the spirit of holiness by resurrection from the dead." (Romans 1:4) "Paul made no recorded attempt to explain Jesus' teaching, to prove from his words and deeds that he was the Messiah…he made no reference to the virgin birth, the miracles, or any salient incident in Jesus' ministry…The Lord Christ, the God-man to be known by faith, replaced the prophet from Nazareth experienced by the disciples…Paul was an apocalypticist, believing that the end was rapidly approaching. He imagined himself carrying the gospel as one of the messengers promised for the end times."[32]

The gospels, written a generation after Paul's letters, share his conviction that Christians are living in the last days. Apocalyptic belief is still the basis and presupposition of Christian preaching. John the Baptist warns, "The ax is already laid at the root of the tree!... The winnowing fork is in his hand, ready to clean out the threshing floor and gather the wheat into his barn, but the husks he will burn with fire that cannot be put out!" (Luke 3:9, 13) Jesus likewise proclaims, "The time allotted has run out and the kingdom has almost arrived! Repent and believe in the good news!" (Mark 1:15)

According to the gospels, the present age will end violently—"As it was in the days of Noah, so it will be at the coming of the Son of Man" (Matthew 24:37)—and "a man's enemies will be members of his own household." (Matthew 10:36) "If anyone comes to me and does not hate father and mother, wife and children, brothers and sisters—yes, even their own life—such a person cannot be my disciple." (Luke 14:26) The nearness of the End cancels out even the most basic family responsibilities—"Follow me and let the dead bury their dead." (Matthew 8:22) There is no time to gather one's possessions (Matthew 24:17-18) or say farewell to those who will not escape, (Luke 9:61-62) "With but few exceptions, studies of Jesus' teaching continue to include a near expectation of the Kingdom as one of the primary ingredients of his message."[33]

Gospel Jesus informs his disciples, "Truly I tell you, you will not finish going through the towns of Israel before the Son of Man comes" (Matthew 10:23), tells a crowd, "some of you who are standing here will not taste death before they see that the kingdom of God has come with power" (Mark 9:1), predicts that "this generation will certainly not pass away until all these things have happened" (Mark 13:30) and warns the Sanhedrin, "I say to all of you: From now on you will see the Son of Man sitting at the right hand of the Mighty One and coming on the clouds of heaven." (Matthew 26:64) As Crawford notes, "there can be no question as to the meaning of these texts. Each is a straightforward announcement of the imminently impending eschatological consummation."[34]

13

The Last Days fantasy is early Christianity's north star, a consistent reference point anchoring belief. The ecstatic prophesying in their gatherings is a sign of the End—"In the last days, God says, I will pour out my spirit on all people. Your sons and daughters will prophesy…" (Acts 2:17). The Revelation to John promises "to show his servants what must soon take place" and concludes with the words, "He who is the faithful witness to all these things says, 'Yes, I am coming soon.' Amen. Come, Lord Jesus." (Revelation 1:1, 22:20) Although Jehovah once spoke through the prophets, "in these last days he has spoken to us by his Son" (Hebrews 1:2) who "was revealed in these last days for your sake." (1 Peter 1:20) The doubt of some simply confirms their belief in the Last Days: "In the last times there will be scoffers who will follow their own ungodly desires" (Jude 1:18) and the disabused who have left the church are merely further proof that the End is upon them—"The spirit clearly says that in latter times some will abandon the faith and follow deceiving spirits and things taught by demons." (1 Timothy 4:1) "There will be terrible times in the last days." (2 Timothy 3:1) The multiplication of Christian sects is proof the "last hour" has arrived: "Dear children, this is the last hour; as you have heard that the antichrist is coming, even now many antichrists have come. This how we know it is the last hour." (1 John 2:18) Wealth is also a sign—"Your gold and silver are corroded. Their corrosion will testify against you and eat your flesh like fire. You have hoarded wealth in the last days." (James 5:3) *Prosperity Gospel preachers beware!*

Despite Jesus' prediction, "this generation will certainly not pass away until all these things have happened. Heaven and earth will pass away but my words will never pass away" (Luke 21:32-33), heaven and earth are still very much here and the apocalypse has not happened. The faithful were assured that "[Christ] will appear a second time, not to bear sin, but to bring salvation to those who are waiting for him," (Hebrews 9:28), but nineteen centuries have passed, and every prediction of the Second Coming, every one of thousands, has been wrong. The faithful were waiting then and are waiting still.

Failed prophecies aside, a Pew Research Center poll done in 2010 found that by 2050 "41% of Americans believe that Jesus Christ definitely (23%) or probably (18%) will have returned to earth...Fully 58% of white evangelical Christians say Christ will return to earth in this period, by far the highest percentage in any religious group...One-in-five religiously unaffiliated Americans also see Christ returning during the next four decades. Americans with no college experience (59%) are much more likely than those with some college experience (35%) or college graduates (19%) to expect Jesus Christ's return. By region, those in the South (52%) are the most likely to predict a Second Coming by 2050."[35]

The salesmen of the apocalypse have never hesitated to capitalize on the credulity of Christians who are convinced Jesus will be back in a hot minute, the religious version of a multi-level marketing scam in which friends and family are urged to buy in. William Miller, a major force in the Adventist movement, foretold the Second Coming would happen on March 21, 1843. Charles Taze Russell, founder of the Bible Student movement, today's Jehovah's Witnesses, predicted the return of Christ would happen in 1874 and again in 1914. William Branham, a Pentecostal faith healer, predicted the Second Coming and the Rapture would occur in 1977. Southern Baptist preacher Pat Robertson predicted the world would end in 1982, but fellow Baptist, Jerry Falwell, opted for 2000. John Hagee, in his "blood moon" prophecy, picked 2014 as The Big One. Harold Camping, a radio show evangelist and indefatigable End Times prophet, predicted Judgment Day would fall on September 26, 1994, then moved the date to September 29 and then to October 2. Undeterred by the failure of his 1994 predictions, Camping famously hit on May 21, 2011 as the date of the Rapture and when that also didn't happen, finally retired from the prophecy business. Grifting off Armageddon is hardly limited to the broadcasting empire of the televangelists. Who can forget prophet Hal Lindsey's internationally famous *The Late Great Planet Earth* that sold tens of millions of copies or Tim LaHaye and Jerry Jenkins masterwork, the *Left*

Behind series of novels, sixteen books set in the "great tribulation" preceding world destruction?

Although End Times fever still rages among many in the evangelical sects, centuries of disconfirmation and unhinged religious frenzy have resulted in a more sedate stance among the mainstream Christian establishment. In the orthodox churches, the Day of Judgment is more often portrayed in works of art than preached in fiery sermons, and in many Protestant churches it has been deferred to some distant and indefinite future. During a national spasm of religious populism, however, history has shown that End Times fervor can reignite. In 2012 a poll by Statista found a full 22% of Americans believe the world will end in their lifetime, a percentage unmatched by any other country except Turkey.[36]

Every day that passes makes belief in "the Rapture" more preposterous. Imagine billions of dead Christians— "the dead in Christ"—shooting out of their graves like horses out of the starting gate at the Kentucky Derby to "meet the Lord in the air." The disillusioned (former?) Christians who posed the question, "Where is this Coming he promised?" had arrived at an inescapable conclusion: both the predictions of Jesus and the assurances of Paul were belied by the passing of time. Jesus and Paul had proven to be false prophets and not just around the edges. *No sane person could take their words in context and honestly claim to believe them.* The disabused among the Christians were hardly the only ones to notice the failure of Christianity's central

17

prophecy. The Roman philosopher, Porphyry of Tyre, declared, "And there is more to Paul's lying: He very clearly says, 'We who are alive.' For it is now three hundred years since he said this and nobody—not Paul and not anyone else—has been caught up in the air."[37] Porphyry knew—over fifteen centuries ago—that Jesus of Nazareth was a handful of dust and his kingdom an empty sack.

That doubt about the Second Coming was widespread is evident from the letter of 1 Clement to Christians living in Corinth, written in the late first century about the same time as Revelation: "Those who are uncertain are miserable, those who doubt in their soul, who say, 'We have heard these things since our fathers' time and look! We have grown old and none of these things has happened!'" But the writer still insists, "You have peered into the Scriptures," and assures his readers, "that nothing mistaken, nor anything falsified has been written in them."[38] The *Didache* (*Teaching*), written around the end of the first century, cautioned its readers, "Do not let your lamps go out, nor your loins be ungirded! The Lord will come with all his saints. Then the world will see the Lord coming on the clouds of heaven!"[39] The faithful waited, loins girded and lamps ablaze, scanning the clouds in vain while the world turned.

"Any cult that survives the failure of its initial prophecy must necessarily modify or scrap its beliefs about the future…by definition no millenarian cult can long survive in its original form…The one undeniable fact is that the

18

attention of the community, and thus of its worship, was entirely on the Imminent End. 'The time is near' and 'Amen, come Lord Jesus' frame the [Revelation] as a whole as much as they express the mood of its hearers."[40] Like the shapeshifting conspiracy theories peddled on social media, non-prophet End Times preachers foretell divine wrath on a nearly weekly basis with no apparent fear their credulous followers will wake up to the fact that nothing ever happens, in part thanks to the open-ended nature of apocalyptic language, not to mention the low expectations of believers. "Apocalyptic symbolism provided more than just protective camouflage for potentially dangerous political statements. It also enhanced the prestige and mystique of these writings and gave them almost unlimited interpretive elasticity. The more obscure the symbolism, the more privileged the reader who understood it and the more elevated the revelation."[41]

That said, at least one of the signs of the End has been completely and indubitably fulfilled: "In their greed these teachers will exploit you with fabricated stories" (2 Peter 2:3), or as the *King James Version* has it, "And through covetousness *shall they with feigned words make merchandise of you.*" American evangelicals have monetized religious dissatisfaction with liberal movements in the present as well as the self-aggrandizing figment that they are vouchsafed unique insight into world events through their parsing of biblical jabberwocky. The *Didache* warned early believers, "But if [a man claiming to be a prophet] has no trade, according to your understanding, see to it that, as a Christian, he shall not live with you idle. But if he will not do it, he is a Christ-monger (*christemporos*). Watch that you keep away from such."[42] After the Eucharist, the Second Coming is Christianity's most lucrative product—being an illusion, it costs little to manufacture and because it never arrives, it costs nothing to ship—and its vast earning potential has been extended indefinitely by the application of an economic theory called *dispensationalism*.

The creature of one John Darby (d. 1882), who received his revelation after falling off a horse, dispensationalism depends on an illiterate reading of scripture that encourages amateur Bible bricoleurs to select suggestive bits of text and cobble them together into oracular utterances only they have the wisdom to interpret. Darby, who believed the invention of the telegraph was a sign of the Impending End, invented a prophecy-generating device that any feeble-minded preacher with a grade school education could easily operate. Biblical literalists from Jehovah's Witnesses to Southern Baptists have assiduously applied themselves to the task, cranking out an endless series of failed predictions. The Jehovah's Witnesses foretold that Armageddon would break out in fury in 1975, and "when 1975 came and went with nothing spectacular having happened," membership in the cult dipped. "Strangely, many Witnesses, particularly those in responsible positions, seemed to suffer from some form of collective amnesia which caused them to act as though the year 1975 had never held any particular importance to them at all."[43] Sadly for the credibility of the various species of Darbyites, for something to count as a sign of the End, the End must eventually occur.

In *When Prophecy Fails*, a sociology classic, Festinger and his co-authors described an End Times cult and drew several conclusions from their study. What if a believer is "presented with evidence, unequivocal and undeniable evidence, that his belief is wrong: what will happen?" Their study concluded that the person might emerge "even more convinced" and "even show a new fervor about convincing and converting other people to his view." Assuming the believer "is a member of a group of convinced persons who can support one another, we would expect the belief to be maintained and the believers to attempt to proselyte or to persuade nonmembers that the belief is correct."[44] Noting that the prediction of the Second Coming of Christ is the prototype of such mass delusions, Festinger cites the Montanist or New Prophecy movement of the second century and the sixteenth-century Anabaptists who "poured greater energy than ever before into obtaining new converts and sending out missionaries, something they never had done before."[45]

Repeated disconfirmation may cause a movement to collapse, as happened with the Millerites of the nineteenth century, but another option exists for overcoming repeated disconfirmation: "The dissonance cannot be eliminated

21

completely by denying or rationalizing the disconfirmation. But there is a way in which the remaining dissonance can be reduced. *If more and more people can be persuaded that the system of belief is correct, then clearly it must, after all, be correct* [emphasis in original]. Consider the extreme case: if everyone in the whole world believed something there would be no question at all as to the validity of this belief."[46] That was the option chosen by the first Christians: "Then the eleven disciples went to Galilee, to the mountain where Jesus had told them to go. When they saw him, they worshiped him; but some doubted. Then Jesus came to them and said, 'All authority in heaven and on earth has been given to me. Therefore go and make disciples of all nations, baptizing them in the name of the Father and of the Son and of the Holy Spirit, and teaching them to obey everything I have commanded you. And surely I am with you always, to the very end of the age.'" (Matthew 28:16-20) Doubting? Having second thoughts about the end of the age? Go convert everyone on earth and teach them to obey everything Jesus commanded. Voilà! Problem solved!

The Roman satirist Lucian describes the career of the religious grifter Peregrinus: "It was then that he learned the wondrous lore of the Christians, by associating with their priests and scribes in Palestine…in a trice he made them all look like children; for he was a prophet, cult-leader, head of a synagogue, and everything, all by himself. He interpreted and explained some of their books and even composed many…Then at length Proteus was apprehended for this and thrown into prison, which itself gave him no little reputation as an asset for his future career and charlatanism and notoriety-seeking he was enamored of…Indeed, people came even from the cities in Asia, sent by the Christians at their common expense, to succor and defend and encourage the hero…So if any charlatan and trickster, able to profit by occasions, comes among them, he quickly acquires sudden wealth by imposing on simple folk."[47] "Lucian's [Peregrinus] is a the first example in literature of an anything-for-profit evangelist who bilks his congregations."[48] As Kannaday notes, it was not just the widows and orphans who were easy marks for fraudsters like Peregrinus. "Even those members of the cult who were viewed as persons of means are portrayed [in *The Passing of Peregrinus*] as fools who will soon be parted from their money. The 'bigwigs of the sect,' as he calls them, come across as impulsive, even whimsical, as they bribe guards for the privilege of sleeping inside the cell with Peregrinus. Lucian's satire, therefore, leaves the impression that Christians are not so much generous as they are gullible, and not so much faithful as they are foolish."[49] "Christians were an easy target for the racketeers of the Roman Empire."[50] Little has changed since Lucian's era; LaHaye, the co-author of the *Left Behind* nonsense, is a Southern Baptist preacher who, "before becoming the champion of Christian America and the apocalypse…made his living as a fortune teller."[51]

As Hoffman points out, the Jewish apocalyptic tradition in which Christianity originated "had been mystically vague, studiously mysterious" regarding the timing of apocalyptic events, and concludes, "Christianity did not so much invent its imprecision as use it to advantage, having mimicked the style of its Jewish prototype...the belief that unfulfilled prophecies had been misread prophecies, provided some consolation to the beleaguered community."[52] By the second generation, prophetic pronunciamento had become increasingly open to interpretation, and warnings about false prophets implied that many had already appeared and there would be many more to come. "So when you see standing in the holy place 'the abomination that causes desolation,' spoken of through the prophet Daniel—let the reader understand—then let those who are in Judea flee to the mountains. Let no one on the housetop go down to take anything out of the house. Let no one in the field go back to get their cloak. How dreadful it will be in those days for pregnant women and nursing mothers! Pray that your flight will not take place in winter or on the Sabbath. For then there will be great distress, unequaled from the beginning of the world until now—and never to be equaled again. If those days had not been cut short, no one would survive, but for the sake of the elect those days will be shortened. At that time if anyone says to you, 'Look, here is the Messiah!' or, 'There he is!' do not believe it. For false messiahs and false prophets will appear and perform great signs and wonders to deceive, if possible, even the elect. See, I have told you ahead of time. So if anyone tells you, 'There he is, out in the wilderness,' do not go out; or, 'Here he is, in the inner rooms,' do not believe it. For as lightning that comes from the east is visible even in the west, so will be the coming of the Son of Man. Wherever there is a carcass, there the vultures will gather." (Matthew 24:15-28)

True to prediction, the vultures continue to gather around the carcass of the Second Coming. The fast-approaching kingdom turned out to be a mirage. As believers imagined themselves rapidly approaching it, the kingdom steadily receded, leaving them to die, one by one, generation after generation, forever. Apocalypticism, the bedrock of Christianity's original theology, is a laughable piece of Levantine folklore.

Part 3: THE RISING SON?

According to Paul, the resurrection of Jesus is the foundation upon which all other Christian claims rested: "If Christ has not been raised, our preaching is useless and so is your faith." (1 Corinthians 15:14) The resurrection is the pivotal event of all time, the hinge on which history turned, and the source of salvation: "if you confess with your mouth that Jesus is Lord and believe in your heart that God raised him from the dead, you will be saved." (Romans 10:9). "Christian faith from its very beginning was firmly rooted in the conviction that God had raised Jesus from the dead…if God did not raise Jesus from the dead, then Christianity has no real basis and is a delusion."[53] "For Christians the resurrection of Jesus constitutes the foundation stone of faith. Apart from the resurrection there is no gospel, no 'good news,' for apart from Easter there is no hope but, as witnessed by the first disciples, only despair."[54] After calling the resurrection "the central miracle in human history," noted apologist Ted Cabal claims his belief is supported by "the testimony of authoritative witnesses…*and the sight of faith rather than empirical perception* (emphasis added)…the amazing certitude of the Holy Spirit through intimate knowledge of a saving relationship with the risen Lord…Christian certainty derives from our personally knowing the risen Lord."[55]

What then, exactly, is the proof of the resurrection, "the central miracle of human history"? Is it "the testimony of authoritative witnesses," or "the sight of faith rather than empirical perception"? How would we distinguish "the sight of faith" from delusion or "the amazing certitude of the Holy Spirit" from a figment of the imagination, a *folie à plusieurs*? Given the crucial importance of the resurrection, the purported guarantee of salvation for all the billions of humans who have ever lived, we might expect—at a bare minimum—multiple eyewitness attestations from *historically confirmed contemporary figures* of Jesus as well as a clear, internally coherent account consistent with other sources. *The resurrection stories meet neither of these criteria.* As a recent examination of miraculous claims, *The Case Against Miracles*, points out, "everything we read in the Gospels *depends entirely on authors who were not there and did not see any of it for themselves* (emphasis in original)…When it comes to the earliest complete Greek manuscripts of the gospel of Mark, and the New Testament as a whole, we have two full manuscripts, the Codex Vaticanus and the Codex Sinaiticus, both dated to the fourth century CE, after three centuries of being copied by hand, which allowed for many variants. So not only do we not have any actual eyewitness testimonies, or eyewitness writings, we don't have any original writings either."[56] In short, the evidence for the resurrection, the basis of the Christian

27

religion, are stories in the gospels *that cannot be corroborated by any other contemporary source.*

According to Mark, the earliest gospel, Jesus foretold his humiliation, crucifixion, and resurrection on three separate occasions: "He then began to teach them that the Son of Man must suffer many things and be rejected by the elders, the chief priests and the teachers of the law, and that he must be killed and after three days rise again."(Mark 8:31) "The Son of Man is to be delivered into men's hands and they will kill him and after three days, he will rise." (Mark 9:31) "They were on their way up to Jerusalem, with Jesus leading the way, and the disciples were astonished, while those who followed were afraid. Again he took the Twelve aside and told them what was going to happen to him. 'We are going up to Jerusalem,' he said, 'and the Son of Man will be delivered over to the chief priests and the teachers of the law. They will condemn him to death and will hand him over to the Gentiles, who will mock him and spit on him, flog him and kill him. Three days later he will rise.'" (Mark 10:32-34)

The gospels tell us that the apostles witness the public resurrection of the son of the widow of Nain (Luke 7:11-17), the raising of Jairus' daughter (Luke 8:49-57), and the dramatic resurrection of Lazarus after three days in the tomb (John 11:1-44), before which Jesus declares, "I am the resurrection and the life." (John 11:25) Yet despite Jesus' detailed predictions and their first-hand experience, the

28

apostles remain thicker than two short planks—they don't understand what Jesus means by 'rising from the dead' (Mark 9:32) even after the Master calls them aside and Jesusplains it all to them. (Mark 10:32)

Did Jesus really call Peter "the rock" (Matthew 16:18) because Peter was the epitome of cluelessness? Jesus heals Peter's mother-in-law (Mark 1:29-31), Peter witnesses Jesus' glorious transfiguration (Mark 9:2), and Peter even walks on water with Jesus. (Matthew 14:22-33) He witnesses Jesus miraculously feed a multitude, cast out hordes of demons, calm a storm, heal the lame and blind, and declares, "You are the Christ, the Son of the living God." (Matthew 16:16) So when some women—*not the apostles*—discover Jesus' tomb is empty, Peter runs to the tomb to investigate, and finding it empty, "he went away, wondering to himself what had happened." (Luke 24:12) What will Peter do next? "'I'm going fishing,' Simon Peter told them, and they said, 'We'll go with you.'" (John 21:3) Because what else would you do when the long-awaited "Christ, the Son of the living God" finally shows up, heals your mother-in-law, performs miracles willy-nilly, gets transfigured along with dignitaries like Moses and Elijah while the voice of God speaks out of a cloud, repeatedly predicts he will rise from the dead *after three days*, and sure enough, *three days later* you find the tomb is empty? *Go fishing apparently*! And so begins a series of mind-boggling non sequiturs, contradictory reports, improbable scenarios, and "proofs" that read like the blithering of lunatics.

Given the critical role of the resurrection, supposedly the foundation of Christian belief, we might expect scores of named witnesses or at least as many who saw the raising of Lazarus. It that's the expectation, we have some bad news and some even worse news. Let's start with the worse news: according to the canonical gospels—the ones the Church decided are the trustworthy *inspired* ones—*not a single person sees Jesus rise from the dead.* Despite his repeated, detailed predictions that he will suffer, die, and rise from the dead three days later, *not even one of Jesus' apostles shows up to watch it happen.* No. One. Sees. Jesus. Come. Back. To. Life. No. One. Sees. Jesus. Leave. The. Tomb.

Contrary to resurrection "experts" such as Gary Habermas, *no one saw Jesus come back to life.* A crowd of people in the street saw the son of the widow of Nain come back to life—"The dead man sat up and began to speak, and Jesus gave him to his mother." (Luke 7:15)—and the disciples as well as her parents witnessed Jairus' daughter come back to life—"He took her by the hand and said to her, *"Talitha koum!"* (which means "Little girl, I say to you, get up!"). Immediately the girl stood up and began to walk around (she was twelve years old). At this they were completely astonished." (Mark 5:41-42) But according to the canonical gospels, *no one saw Jesus come back to life.*

30

Lazarus' family and a crowd of mourners saw Lazarus leave his tomb—"Jesus called in a loud voice, 'Lazarus, come out!' The dead man came out…" (John 11:43-44) But according to the gospels the church considers authentic, *no one saw Jesus come out of his tomb.* In short, despite the claims of apologists, *not a single person witnessed Jesus come back to life or leave his tomb. There were no "eyewitnesses" to Jesus' resurrection.* To make such a claim is to effectively rewrite the gospel stories to agree with an *a priori* belief, to make the "evidence" fit a presupposed conclusion. According to a well-known quote by Habermas, "The closer the time between the event and testimony about it, the more reliable the witness," but the New Testament reports no witnesses who saw Jesus come back to life or a single witness who saw Jesus leave the tomb; the resurrection was not an "event" anyone had actually seen. At some point some Christians became convinced that Jesus had returned based on appearances, visions, or apparitions, but millions have experienced appearances of the deceased and very few are convinced any of them really returned from the dead.

Lest anyone think that's already about as bad as it can get, brace yourself. When some of the women who followed Jesus visit the tomb and discover it empty, Mark tells us, "And they left the tomb running, for they were trembling and beside themselves, and they said nothing to anyone because they were afraid." (Mark 16:8) For whatever reason that's how the manuscripts of Mark considered most reliable leave matters, with no prior belief, *stated or implied*, that his disciples expected to find Jesus risen from the dead and his tomb empty. Now clearly Matthew, Luke, and John can't let the story end this way, but when they polish it up theologically, they just introduce even more incoherence, confusion, and contradiction.

A comparison of Paul's explanation of resurrection bodies with the proof of resurrection offered in the gospel of Luke is an example of murky resurrection theology. Paul's letter, written a generation before the gospels, assures believers "it is sown a natural body, it is raised a *spiritual body (sōma pneumatikon)*" and tells us that Christ, "the last Adam, became *a life-giving spirit (pneuma zōopoion)*." (1 Corinthians 15:44) When Luke tries to demonstrate that Jesus is back from the dead, Jesus appears suddenly in the apostles midst with predictable results: "They were startled and frightened, thinking they saw a *ghost (pneuma)*. He said to them, 'Why are you troubled, and why do doubts rise in your minds? Look at my hands and my feet. It is I myself! Touch me and see; a *ghost (pneuma)* does not have flesh and bones, as you see I have.'" (Luke 24:37-39, *New International Version*) The translation of *pneuma* in the *New International Version* is completely consistent with ancient and modern expectations of ghost behavior—ghosts appear out of nowhere. The problem is that Luke 24 doesn't use a general term for ghost such as *phantasma*—"It's a *ghost*

32

(*phantasma*)," they said, and cried out in fear." (Matthew 14:26) Luke has Jesus tell his disciples a *spirit* (*pneuma*) "does not have flesh and bones, as you see I have." If Jesus was raised with a spiritual body and became a *spirit* (*pneuma*) as Paul claims, how does an apparition with flesh and bones like "a natural body" prove the resurrection, particularly when Jesus stipulates, "a spirit (*pneuma*) does not have flesh and bones, as you see I have"? Little wonder Jesus' disciples were "troubled."

According to all four gospels, women were the first to find the empty tomb. And according to the gospels, Jesus taught "plainly," "openly"—the word Mark uses is *parrhesia*, which means "unambiguously"—that he would rise from the dead after three days. When Peter tries to tell him that's nonsense, Jesus rebukes him in the strongest possible terms, the famous "Get behind me, Satan!" logion. (Matthew 16:23) When John tells the resurrection tale, the woman who finds the tomb unoccupied proposes a natural— *not a supernatural*—explanation for the missing corpse: "They have taken my Lord away and I don't know where they've put him!" (John 20:13) In short, the iconic empty tomb, Men in White notwithstanding, did not prove to the women that Jesus had risen from the dead. To the contrary, it became a source of fear and confusion. And even though a "young man" in the empty tomb instructs the women, "tell his disciples and Peter, 'He is going ahead of you into

Galilee. There you will see him, just as he told you,'" the women "said nothing to anyone." (Mark 16:7-8)

Much ink has been spilled, particularly by feminist scholars, about the women witnesses to the resurrection, the first "Easter preachers," but as already noted, no one saw the resurrection according to the canonical gospels and the empty tomb inspired, not reassurance and consolation, but fear and confusion. The male disciples, who "have left everything" to follow Jesus (Mark 10:28) are unimpressed with the women's discovery. By Luke's account the Eleven Amigos were having none of it: "After returning from the tomb they reported all these things to the Eleven and all the others. The women were Mary Magdalene, Joanna, and Mary, the mother of James, and the other women with them who told the apostles these things. *But their words seemed like nonsense to them and they didn't believe the women.*" (Luke 24:9-11)

If Jesus taught *emphatically* that he'd be back among the living three days after his crucifixion, and raised others from the dead as proof that he was "the resurrection and the life," why didn't the disciples gather at his tomb in anticipation of the resurrection, and why, given the witness of the women and the discovery of the empty tomb, were they still unconvinced? Is it possible Jesus expected to eat the next compulsory Passover with his disciples in a miraculously restored kingdom—"I will not drink from this fruit of the vine from now on until that day when I drink it new with you

in my Father's kingdom" (Matthew 26:29; Luke 22:16)—
and the resurrection stories are incoherent back-formations
designed to account for a shocking and unexpected turn of
events, Jesus' arrest and execution?

According to the gospel of John, this is what happened
after Jesus expired: "Later, Joseph of Arimathea, who was a
secret disciple of Jesus for fear of the Jews, asked Pilate if
he might take Jesus' body and Pilate consented, so he came
and took his body. Nicodemus, who earlier had come to see
Jesus by night, brought a mixture of myrrh and aloes, around
seventy-five pounds. Then they took Jesus' body and
wrapped it in linen cloth together with the spices as is the
Jewish burial custom. There was a garden in the place he was
crucified and in the garden was a new tomb in which no one
had ever been placed. Because it was the Jewish Preparation
Day, and because the tomb was nearby, they laid Jesus
there." (John 19::38-42)

Several features of this short story are improbable, flatly
contradict the timeline of events in other gospels, or raise
even more questions than it answers, starting with Joseph of
Arimathea who Mark describes as a respected *bouleutēs* or
"council member," (Mark 15:43) a voting member of the
Sanhedrin, the Jewish court that condemned Jesus for
blasphemy. (Mark 14:64) According to Mark, the vote to
hand Jesus over to the Roman authorities, essentially a death
sentence, was *unanimous* as required by Jewish law: "They
all condemned him as worthy of death." (Mark 14:64)

Would Joseph, a member of the court, vote to condemn Jesus despite being a secret disciple?

If, as John claims, Joseph and Nicodemus wrapped Jesus' corpse in linen on the Jewish day of Preparation, *the day before Passover*, then their contact with a dead body made them ceremonially unclean and disqualified them from celebrating Passover—"But some of them could not celebrate the Passover on that day because they were ceremonially unclean on account of a dead body." (Numbers 9:6) For that matter, how likely is it that Joseph would enter Pilate's praetorium, the hall of judgment, to ask for Jesus' body if mere contact with a Gentile would make him unclean and prevent him from participating in a major Jewish festival? (John 18:28) If the gospel account is accurate, Joseph was doubly disqualified from observing Passover due to touching a corpse and rubbing elbows with Gentiles. How likely is it that a prominent Jewish official, a member of the Sanhedrin, would disregard a clear command from the Tanakh: "[Passover] is day you are to commemorate; for the generations to come you shall celebrate it as a festival to the Lord—a lasting ordinance." (Exodus 12:14).

John's brief account manages to introduce a further problem, a glaring calendar discrepancy. If Jesus was arrested, tried, and executed the day before Passover began—the trial occurred on "the day of Preparation of the Passover; it was about noon" (John 19:14)—then it was clearly impossible for Jesus to celebrate Passover with his

36

disciples as described by Mark: "The disciples left, went to the city, and found everything just as Jesus had told them, and they prepared the Passover meal." (Mark 14:16) Jesus may have worked miracles, but he cannot have died the day *before* Passover and still have celebrated Passover—dead in one version of the story but still alive in another.

Scholars who have examined the resurrection stories in the light of Roman and Jewish accounts have identified additional problems. Rome "typically denied burial to victims of crucifixion" and "Rabbinic law specifies that criminals may not be buried in tombs."[57] Despite nearly contemporary records claiming many thousands were executed by crucifixion in Judea, "neither biblical nor extra-biblical texts prior to the turn of the first century furnish anything like the description of crucifixion and the death of Jesus that is so commonly assumed in scholarly texts; ancient accounts of crucifixion…are rare, their descriptions are vague, and the New Testament authors offer very few details concerning the form of Jesus's death."[58] Archaeologists have recovered only a single clear specimen from a crucified man found in a burial cave at Giv'at ha Mirvar, a heel bone pierced by a nail, forensic evidence that suggests the crucified were rarely buried in tombs. A few other specimens exist for which death by crucifixion has been proposed, but expert opinion is divided. If the crucified were more commonly tied than nailed, identifying victims of crucifixion would prove much more difficult.

In addition to the contradictions and incoherence of the resurrection accounts, the gospels themselves refute the claim that Jesus received burial: "Pilate wrote a title also, and put it on the cross. And there was written, JESUS OF NAZARETH, THE KING OF THE JEWS." (John 19:19) The gospel accounts agree that Jesus' immediate followers thought he would restore the ancient Jewish kingdom—the Passover crowds gathered to see Jesus proclaim, "Blessed is the king of Israel!" (John 12:13) and as Jesus approached the holy city we are told "the people thought that the kingdom of God was going to appear at once." (Luke 19:11) What did the disciples understand by "the kingdom of God"? In this case at least, the Bible has the answer: "Do not leave Jerusalem, but wait for the gift my Father promised, which you have heard me speak about...Then they gathered around him and asked him, "Lord, are you at this time going to restore the kingdom to Israel?" (Acts 1:4-6) Regarding the messianic expectations of Jesus' contemporaries, historian Geza Vermes notes, "the Messiah...was expected to be a king of David's lineage, victor over the Gentiles, saviour and restorer of Israel."[59]

Asserting Rome's unchallenged authority was Pontius Pilate's chief role as the Roman administrator of Judea, to ensure by force if necessary that Rome's authority remained unchallenged. The Jewish leaders John claims spoke at Jesus' trial have it exactly right: "If you let this man go, you are no friend of Caesar. Anyone who claims to be a

38

king opposes Caesar." They then acknowledge a basic fact of Judean realpolitik: "We have no king but Caesar." (John 19:12, 19) At one point Luke's gospel mentions "there were some present at that time who told Jesus about the Galileans whose blood Pilate had mixed with their sacrifices." (Luke 13:1) The gospel writer describes Pilate as a man quite willing to slaughter Jews in the sacred precinct of the Temple—the place where Jews offered sacrifices to God— but when confronted with an aspiring King of the Jews in opposition to Caesar, suddenly becomes the very picture of sweet reason and meek acquiescence and suggests Jesus be freed.

The *titulus crucis*, JESUS OF NAZARETH, THE KING OF THE JEWS, is an official indictment, the formal charge specifying why Jesus is condemned to crucifixion. Public crucifixion was a warning; "the display of the condemned was important not only communicating the dishonour and degradation of the victim but in instilling both fear and delight in visitors, in asserting the power of the state…a naked victim displayed in a prominent place reinforced the humiliation of the procedure; that denial of burial compounded such a humiliation…the corpses of executed individuals were closely guarded by soldiers to ensure they did not receive a burial…Denial of burial was ultimately an extension of the damnation the victim received in life."[60] The display of the crucified, stained by their own blood and feces, open wounds seething with maggots, their bodies covered with flies, were a gruesome warning to others—in the case of Jesus, a warning to other would-be kings of the Jews.

Comparing the story as Luke tells it with Matthew's version strikes more discordant notes. In Luke's resurrection tale, the Men in White have to remind the half-witted women of Jesus' prediction: "Remember, as he said to you when he was in Galilee, the Son of Man must be betrayed into the hands of sinful men and be crucified and on the third day be raised." (Luke 24:6-7) Strangely enough, the "sinful men" who crucified Jesus easily recall his prediction *without being reminded* by any Men in White: "Sir, we remember that fraud said while still alive, 'After three days I will rise.' Therefore, order that the tomb be made secure so his disciples don't come and steal him and tell the people he's risen." (Matthew 27:63-64) Why do Jesus' mortal enemies recall his prediction better than his closest disciples?

This brings us around yet again to the women who came to the tomb, days after his death, "to anoint Jesus' body." (Mark 16:1) By John's account, Joseph of Arimathea and Nicodemus had already embalmed Jesus' body and wrapped it in linen "in accordance with Jewish burial customs." (John 19:40) Within a similar time frame, Lazarus' corpse had already started to stink. (John 11:39) Were the women intending to unwrap a bloating body and smear ointment on it? Historian Lane Fox notes the likelihood that "women were a clear majority" in the early church, and of the writings of Roman critics observes, "I was a well-established theme...that strange teachings appealed to leisured women who had just enough culture to admire it and not enough education to exclude it."[61] Catherine Kroeger approaches the issue of women witnesses from the standpoint of "the socio-religious world of [Greco-Roman] women" that addresses the social strata of Christian women specifically: "Neither is it surprising that women who lacked any sort of formal education flocked to the cults that were despised by the intellectuals."[62] Women in the ancient world "were expressly targeted as unreliable witnesses, possessed, fanatical, sexual libertines, domineering of or rebellious toward their husbands,"[63] and by the end of the first century Christian estimation of women appears little better: "I do not permit a woman to teach or to exercise authority over a man...[Younger women] get into the habit of being idle and gadding about from house to house. Not only do they become idlers, but also busybodies who talk nonsense, saying things they ought not." (1 Timothy 2:12, 5:13) In Paul's list of witnesses to the resurrection, which predates the gospels by decades, women are notable for their absence.

In Matthew, early Christianity's favorite gospel, the author abandons all pretense of historical reportage, crashes through the guardrails, and takes his readers off-roading through the wilderness of the imagination. Who the author of this high-on-Jesus joy ride really was is unknown, but for convenience sake we'll follow convention and call him

"Matthew." A hint of how crazy this is about to get is indicated by Matthew's reworking of Mark's story of the women at the tomb—Matthew uses Mark as his primary source, quoting or paraphrasing around ninety-five percent of Mark's gospel and following his timeline. Here is Mark's opening of his story: "[The women] began saying to one another, 'Who will roll away the stone from the entrance of the tomb for us?" (Mark 16:3) Here is Matthew's solution to the women's doorman problem: "Behold! A great earthquake occurred because an angel of the Lord descended from heaven and approaching them, he rolled the stone away and sat upon it. His appearance was like lightening and his clothing as white as snow." (Matthew 28:12-13)

Matthew's moment of Jesus' death is no less lurid: "After crying out once more, he gave up his spirit. And behold! The curtain in the Temple was torn in half from top to bottom, and the earth shook, and the rocks were split, and the tombs were opened, and the bodies of many holy people who had died were raised, and when they came out of their tombs after his resurrection, they went into the holy city and were seen by many." (Matthew 27:50-53) Did you *behold* all that earthshaking melodrama? Among the seismic prodigies that accompanied Jesus' final moments *on Friday*, the tombs opened up, and many dead were raised, but they just hung out in their tombs *until Sunday*, "after his resurrection," before walking into Jerusalem where they "were seen by many." Oddly enough, holy zombies doing a march on

42

Jerusalem is unmentioned in the other gospels or by any histories of the era. If a hoard of dead people proved Jesus had risen from the tomb, why didn't Jesus Himself show up in Jerusalem accompanied by angels and dressed in shining raiment? After all, Jesus promised the court, "You will see the Son of Man seated at the right hand of power and coming with the clouds of heaven!" (Mark 14:62) Why didn't Jesus appear post-mortem to his persecutors and settle the question of his resurrection then and there, once and for all as he promised at his trial?

By the time Matthew wrote his moonbat revision of Mark, opponents of the Jesus cult may have proposed what scholars call "the stolen body hypothesis" to counter the resurrection claim, hence Matthew's inclusion of another narrative disaster. In this episode, the high priests and Pharisees approach Pilate, remind him that Jesus will be back in three days, and request "the tomb be made secure for three days so his disciples won't come and steal his body and tell the people he's been raised from the dead" and Pilate obligingly says, "Take a guard and go make the tomb as secure as you know how" so they "secured the tomb by sealing the stone and posting a guard." In the meanwhile, the woman go to the tomb, see Jesus outside the tomb, and are instructed to tell the disciples Jesus will meet them in Galilee. "While [the women] were on their way, some of the guard went to the city and reported everything that had happened to the high priests. After meeting with the elders, they hatched a plan to give the soldiers a sum of money, telling them, 'Say his disciples came by night and stole him while we were sleeping and if this gets back to the governor, we'll cover for you so you won't have to worry.' So the soldiers took the money and did what they were told and this story spread among the Jews up till now." (Matthew 27:62-64, 28:11-15) If the soldiers revealed some evidence of the resurrection to the Jewish authorities that was so compelling the authorities bribed the soldiers not to repeat it, why don't the gospels just tell us what that evidence was? If the gospel writer knew the details of this alleged transaction, why did he leave out the most important piece of information?

Matthew had already established that the stone covering the entrance to the tomb was so heavy it took an angel to move it, but now a gaggle of Galilean hillbillies manage to remove the seal, roll the stone aside, and carry off a corpse in the dead of night without waking any of the soldiers guarding the tomb. A problem that would occur to anyone familiar with Roman-occupied Palestine concerns the identity of the soldiers. Although the Temple had a police force under the command of the High Priest, the force described in Matthew answered to Pilate, the Roman governor. Who were the soldiers? The Greek text of Matthew uses the term *stratiōtēs*, the usual word for *soldier*; the same term, *stratiōtai, soldiers*, is used in Matthew 27:27 of the Roman troops who mocked and humiliated Jesus before crucifying him. Matthew also uses a Greek loan word, *koustōdia*, from the Latin *custodia*, a military guard, and since the guard has been sent on Pilate's orders, logically a picket of Roman soldiers.

Would a Roman military detachment authorized by a Roman official have reported back to a *Jewish* priest? What fate would await Roman soldiers who reported their missions had failed because they were asleep on watch duty? The Roman military practiced *decimation* as punishment for insubordination and dereliction of duty—his fellow soldiers killed every tenth man in a unit selected for the punishment of decimation. Given the stringent discipline of Roman forces generally, particularly those stationed in a hostile province such as Judea, what is the likelihood a detachment of Roman troops would lie to their commander, and by extension the governor of the province, in return for a bribe if discovery would result in summary execution? Clearly, as pointed out by later Roman critics, the gospels were written for the edification of credulous yokels eager to be titillated by pious miracle stories. The people for whom the gospels were composed not only accepted the fantastic and improbable at face value, they expected it. As Jesus himself complained, "Unless you see signs and wonders, you will never believe." (John 4:48) For most ancient listeners, sexing up a story with angels, earthquakes, visions, and the supernatural in general made it *more believable*, not less. Who wants to read a ho-hum Bible story in which nothing incredible happens?

The gospel stories generally are simply hopeless. In Luke's story the sun stops shining during Jesus' crucifixion. Luke's text (23:45) specifies that it happened due to *an eclipse (eklipontos)*—"an astronomical impossibility…since Passovers occur at full moon and solar eclipses occur only at a new moon…by way of defense [the apologist] Origen insisted that secret enemies of the church had introduced the notion of an eclipse into the text to make it vulnerable to a show of reason."[64] According to Matthew, "from noon until three in the afternoon darkness came over the land," (Matthew 27:45) but as the ancients knew, solar eclipses are brief, rarely lasting much over seven minutes.

The first mention of the resurrection that has survived until the present comes, not from the gospels, but from a letter written by Paul of Tarsus decades before the first gospel. Paul appears to have no interest whatever in the 'historical Jesus' that has occupied generations of scholars— "Even though we have known Christ according to the flesh, we know him so no more." (2 Corinthians 5:16) Paul never met Jesus in the flesh and has no interest in his earthly career. He never mentions any of Jesus' exorcisms, healings, or even feats like the resurrection of Lazarus. For Paul, Jesus only gets interesting once he's risen from the dead, but even here his attention to detail is sketchy. Paul says Jesus "was raised on the third day according to the scriptures" (1 Corinthians 15:4) but there are no scriptures that foretell a messiah who appears at long last only to be arrested and executed, much less a messiah who rises from the grave after three days.

After his visionary conversion on the road to Damascus recounted in Acts—an event Paul never mentions in his letters—Paul didn't immediately hie himself to Jerusalem to meet Jesus' family, retrace the Master's steps, or sit at the feet of the apostles who had accompanied the Lord. *Au contraire*, "I did not go up to Jerusalem to see those who were apostles before I was, but I went to Arabia. Later I returned to Damascus." (Galatians 1:17) When, after a number of years, Paul decided God had "set me apart from my mother's womb" to preach Jesus (Galatians 1:15), he says in no uncertain terms, "I want you to know, brothers, that the gospel I preached is not of human origin. I did not receive it from any man, nor was I taught it; rather I received it by revelation from Jesus Christ." (Galatians 1:11-12) In short, like the writers of the later gospels, Paul had a casual relationship at best with the 'historical' Jesus.

Here is Paul's remarkably brief description of Jesus' resurrection: "I passed on to you as of primary importance what I also received, that Christ died for our sins according to the scriptures, and that he was buried and that he was raised on the third day according to the scriptures, and that he appeared to Cephas, then to the twelve, then he appeared to more than five hundred brothers at one time, the greater number of whom remain until now but some have died. Then he appeared to James, then to all the apostles. Last of all he

47

appeared to me, as to one born before his time." (1 Corinthians 15:3-8)

Paul makes no mention of an empty tomb, or of women witnesses, or of Men in White. Instead, "more than five hundred brothers"—who remain mysteriously unmentioned by the gospels written later—see Jesus "at one time." Who were the "more than five hundred brothers"? What did they see? When and where did they see it? Your guess is as good as anyone else's including the "experts." This passing mention is the last we hear about them.

Christian apologists have cranked out mountains of verbiage attempting to paper over the cracks in this narrative and harmonize it with the gospels, but the opinion of Gregory Riley neatly summarizes the conclusion of mainstream New Testament scholars: "a simple comparison of the Gospels and 1 Corinthians 15 shows the two traditions cannot be reconciled."[65] Even apologetic writers are forced to admit, "Paul's list of appearances in 1 Corinthians and the resurrection narratives in the gospels are remarkably—and puzzlingly—ill-matched." [66]

To the dismay of the true believer, it may be pointed out that *disbelief in the resurrection begins in the New Testament itself* and begins decades before the composition of the gospels: "But if it is preached that Christ has been raised from the dead, *how can some of you say there is no resurrection of the dead?*" (1 Corinthians 15:12) "Surely the very fact that Paul placed a lengthy list of eyewitnesses of the appearances of the risen Jesus at the very beginning of the whole discussion is most easily explained by the suggestion that the apostle feared some of his addressees entertained doubts on this matter."[67] Given that there were grounds for doubt even among the "eyewitnesses," we may safely conclude that the gospel reports of the resurrection were composed primarily with apologetic, not historical, intent. Some have argued that the whole project of trying to ground the resurrection in history be abandoned. Quoting William Farmer, Sider says, "[Farmer] has recently argued vehemently that the only kind of evidence for the resurrection the church has ever had—and should have ever desired—is the inner experience of justification by faith alone...Barth and Bultmann, too, are typical of many, who, albeit in somewhat different ways, reject any citation of historical evidence to support the church's belief in Jesus' resurrection."[68] So we're back to "the sight of faith" that could prove literally anything to anyone inclined to believe it.

According to Luke, the male disciples who went to the tomb "did not see Jesus." (Luke 24:24) The tactile Jesus who later appears to them may be an attempt to "counter the idea that the risen Jesus was some type of ghost or phantasm."[69] So who or what, exactly, did Paul and other followers of Jesus see? The Roman philosopher Celsus wrote a lengthy refutation of the Jesus Cult, *Logos Alēthēs*, *True Doctrine*, late in the second century, a work later destroyed by

Christians and known today only from quotations in Origen's belated response, *Contra Celsum*. Pointing out the phantasmal qualities of the post-resurrection appearances, Celsus says that Jesus manifested to his disciples "like a ghost hovering before their perception"[70]—Celsus' vocabulary suggests something unsubstantial drifting before one's vision. As historian J.D. Crossan observes, "apparitions of Jesus do not constitute resurrection. They constitute apparitions, no more and no less."[71]

Several features of the resurrection tales read like ghost stories. Like a ghost, Jesus suddenly appears and disappears—"Though the doors were locked, Jesus came and stood among them" (John 20:26); "he became invisible to them." (Luke 24:31) His sudden apparitions provoke fear: "While they were talking about these things, he stood in their midst and said to them, 'Peace be with you.' But they were alarmed and afraid, thinking they were seeing a spirit." (Luke 24:36-37)

I have argued elsewhere that the details of Jesus' post-mortem appearances in Luke and John are likely derived from Greco-Roman ghost lore.[72] In the era in which Christianity appeared a clear majority accepted visions and the appearance of ghosts as real events and lived in the expectation of omens, prophetic dreams, and other close encounters of the supernatural kind. Like many people of the present, they were primed for self-delusion, expecting the inexplicable, accepting the uncanny. Given the mass of contradictions and implausibility of the resurrection stories, who bears the burden of proof, the apologists who claim the gospels record eyewitness history, or the skeptic who can point to modern "sightings" such as apparitions of the Virgin Mary? Moving from the visionary experience of the first Christians, the gospel stories are sequels, examples of *retconning, retroactive continuity,* revisions that alter or differently interpret the details of the tale as originally told.

In Matthew's sequel the eleven remaining apostles meet Jesus on a mountain in Galilee where Jesus gives them the Great Commission to convert the world. In that famous passage we're told, "they fell to their knees before him, *but some doubted.*" (Matthew 28:17) Lest we suppose that "some doubted" part doesn't still have Christian heads spinning like tops in the present age, do an online search of "some doubted verse"—when I did, I got *14,700,000 hits* which seems like a lot of Jesusplaining over something believers are supposedly certain about.

Part 4: JESUS FAMILY VALUES

It is difficult to read the historian Josephus' account of the first Roman-Jewish War without wondering if many of the characters he describes were not simply sociopaths and madmen, clinically insane. It would appear a similar notion may have crossed Josephus' mind as he recorded his history: "*Deceivers (planoi)* and frauds, under the pretense of divine inspiration, instigated revolutionary changes and persuaded the multitude to act like madmen and led them out into the desert under the belief that God would there display signs of their deliverance."[73] The Jewish leaders apply the term *deceiver* to Jesus: "while he was still alive that *deceiver (planos)* said, 'After three days I will rise again.'" (Matthew 27:63)

The church historian Eusebius recounts the appearance of "a certain Jesus by name…a commoner from the countryside" who, four years prior to the outbreak of the Roman-Jewish War (66-73 CE), began incessantly preaching imminent judgment on Jerusalem. Regarded by the religious leaders as demon-possessed, Jesus son of Ananias was hauled before the Roman governor Albinus and flogged to the bone with whips.[74] According to some manuscripts of Josephus' *Jewish War* on which Eusebius' account was based, Albinus finally declared the wretched man insane and released him.

Jesus son of Ananias bears more than a passing resemblance to Jesus of Nazareth, another rustic from the hinterlands—"No prophet comes from Galilee! (John 7:52)—who likewise prophesied a series of woes on Jerusalem—"Not one stone here will be left on another; every one will be thrown down." (Mark 13:2) Like Jesus son of Ananias, Jesus of Nazareth was also considered insane or in league with the demons: "When his family heard about this, they went to take charge of him, for they said, 'He is out of his mind.' And the teachers of the law who came down from Jerusalem said, 'He is possessed by Beelzebul! By the prince of demons he is driving out demons.'" (Mark 3:21-22) Jesus of Nazareth was also delivered up to a Roman governor by the Jewish authorities, also flogged, but was crucified rather than released. The similarities between the two Jesuses is not coincidental; Jerusalem "was the eschatological centre of the world, the destination of the homecoming Diaspora and of the pilgrimages of the nations, the place of the coming of the messiah...the place of judgment of Gehinnom and the metropolis of his coming kingdom" as well as "eschatologically motivated attempts as rebellion."[75] It would appear that being a persistent and obnoxious religious pest resulted in a vicious flogging in the case of Jesus son of Ananias and an even worse punishment in the case of Jesus of Nazareth who drew excited crowds— the Jewish authorities "were afraid of the crowd because the people held that he was a prophet." (Matthew 21:46)

For the attentive reader of the gospels, Jesus of Nazareth sounds like a classic case of dissociative identity disorder, a person in whom two or more distinct personalities coexist. The Jesus Christians love to quote—"I tell you, love your enemies and pray for those who persecute you." (Matthew 5:44)—has a darker other self: "If anyone comes to me and does not hate father and mother, wife and children, brothers and sisters—yes, even their own life—such a person cannot be my disciple." (Luke 14:26) "For I have come to turn a man against his father, a daughter against her mother, a daughter-in-law against her mother-in-law. A man's enemies will be members of his own household." (Matthew 10:35-36) "I have come to set the world on fire and I wish it were already burning!" (Luke 12:49, *New Living Translation*) Loving shepherd or determined arsonist? As David Madison among others has pointed out, Jesus could talk any rational person out of Christianity.[76]

Gospel Jesus has some pretty extreme solutions to common situations. "If your right eye causes you to stumble, gouge it out and throw it away. It is better for you to lose one part of your body than for your whole body to be thrown into hell. And if your right hand causes you to stumble, cut it off and throw it away. It is better for you to lose one part of your body than for your whole body to go into hell…If your hand or your foot causes you to stumble, cut it off and throw it away. It is better for you to enter life maimed or crippled than to have two hands or two feet and be thrown into eternal

54

fire. And if your eye causes you to stumble, gouge it out and throw it away. It is better for you to enter life with one eye than to have two eyes and be thrown into the fire of hell." (Matthew 5:29-30, 18:8-9)

Jesus' command to mutilate oneself hardly stops with an eye, hand, or foot however. "For there are eunuchs who have been so from birth, and there are eunuchs who have been made eunuchs by men, and there are eunuchs who have made themselves eunuchs for the sake of the kingdom of heaven. Let the one who is able to receive this receive it." (Matthew 19:12, *English Standard Version*.) The suggestion that believers who are "able to receive" self-castration should do it—after all, less is more—is a bridge too far for some translators who opt for *interpretation* rather than translate this troublesome passage: "there are those who choose to live like eunuchs" (*New International Version*); "Others stay single in order to serve God better" (*Contemporary English Version*); "others are celibate because they have made themselves that way" (*International Standard Version*). Apparently the translators of these dishonest renditions think the Son of God, who "knew what [men] were thinking" before they said anything (Luke 6:8), didn't know the difference between castration and celibacy. Jesus isn't talking about men who are confirmed bachelors. Jesus is talking about men castrated by other men— "eunuchized by men" (*eunouchisthēsan hupo tōn anthrōpōn*)—as well as men who "eunuchized themselves"

55

(*eunouchisan heautous*). So much for "be happy with the way God made you."

Surely no rational man would think himself spiritually elevated because he had removed his own testicles! That reaction would be true if we were talking about rational people, but we aren't. We're talking about early Christians. Self-castration has never been a subject Christian scholars were eager to address and long received "only passing notice," as a recent writer observes. "These studies, like the orthodox treatises from which the evidence must be drawn, tend to marginalize self-castration as a rare act on the 'lunatic fringe' of early Christian asceticism...Though testimony is scanty, sources from the fourth century indicate that by then self-castration had become a real problem in the nascent Church...by which time an ascetic movement that included not merely renunciation of marriage but also extreme forms of self-mortification had become influential and widespread in Christian communities. To judge from the sources, the numbers of Christians who had castrated themselves had by that time become rather conspicuous."[77] The Council of Nicaea, convened in 325 CE to address the Arian heresy, also excluded the self-castrated from the priesthood, a decision reiterated in the Apostolic Constitutions of 375 CE.

The church historian Eusebius said that Origen, a prominent Christian figure of the second century, castrated himself in his teens, the action of "an immature mind," yet

56

praised as an act "of faith and self-control."[78] Justin Martyr, the early apologist, applauded a young Alexandrian convert who petitioned the Roman governor to give a surgeon permission to castrate him.[79] According to the fourth century bishop, Epiphanius of Salamis, a Christian sect called the Valesians were mostly self-made eunuchs. Epiphanius also charged them with forcing castration on others: "And not only do they impose this discipline on their own disciples; it is widely rumored that they have often made this disposition of strangers when they were passing through and accepted their hospitality. They seize them when they come inside, bind them on their backs to boards, and perform the castration by force."[80] A sympathetic reading of the "theme of self-dismemberment" construes it as metaphor, "another of Matthew's extreme illustrations by which he summons his readers toward wholehearted devotion to Jesus so that they might enter his kingdom…the willingness to sacrifice essential present-age concerns" which included "a spouse and children."[81]

Wives and children are never mentioned among Jesus' entourage, but children are named among those his followers might abandon: "'Truly I tell you,' Jesus replied, 'no one who has left home or brothers or sisters or mother or father *or children* or fields for me and the gospel will fail to receive a hundred times as much in this present age: homes, brothers, sisters, mothers, *children* and fields—along with persecutions—and in the age to come eternal life.'" (Mark

10:29-30) Did Jesus leave his own "children, brothers and sisters"? Did he consider the loss of family members, brothers, sisters, mothers and children, as the equivalent of losing a field? As in any cult, *only true believers are family*: "Pointing to his disciples, he said, 'Here are my mother and my brothers. For whoever does the will of my Father in heaven is my brother and sister and mother.'" (Matthew 12:49-50)

In addition to having some serious issues with family and sex, Jesus' mood can turn on a dime. "I am the good shepherd. The good shepherd lays down his life for the sheep" (John 10:11) and "this is the will of him who sent me, that I shall lose none of all those he has given me, but raise them up at the last day" (John 6:39), but "many will say to me on that day, 'Lord, Lord, did we not prophesy in your name and in your name drive out demons and in your name perform many miracles?' Then I will tell them plainly, 'I never knew you. Away from me, you evildoers!'" (Matthew 7:22-23) If you love him, he is all you will ever need, but don't make Jesus hurt you!

Jesus' extended "family of believers throughout the world" (1 Peter 5:9) was not without its internal issues. Paul complains, "if someone comes to you and preaches a Jesus other than the Jesus we preached, or if you receive a different spirit from the Spirit you received, or a different gospel from the one you accepted, you put up with it easily enough." (2 Corinthians 11:4) The church is plagued by "false apostles, deceitful workers, masquerading as apostles of Christ" (2 Corinthians 11:13) and "false believers had infiltrated our ranks" (Galatians 2:4) as well. The faithful are warned, "even now many antichrists have come. This is how we know it is the last hour. *They went out from us*, but they did not really belong to us." (1 John 2:18-19) From its very beginning Christianity was riven with dissension and competition. Those out of favor are tossed out—"hand this man over to Satan for the destruction of the flesh." (1 Corinthians 5:5) The faithful are admonished, "have confidence in your leaders and submit to their authority" (Hebrews 13:17) and are warned: "We will be ready to punish every act of disobedience, once your obedience is complete." (2 Corinthians 10:6) The language of early Christianity is the language of a cult.

Paul (or his disciples) clearly considered himself to be Jesus' chief spokesman: "You heard about the mission of God's grace *entrusted to me on your behalf*, the mystery *revealed to me* by revelation...you will be able to *understand my insight* into the mystery of Christ that in previous generations was not made known to the sons of men as it has now been revealed in spirit to his holy apostles and prophets." (Ephesians 3:2-5) "God was pleased *to reveal his Son in me so that I might preach him* among the Gentiles." (Galatians 1:15-16) The preaching of Paul also includes this revelation: "it is disgraceful for a woman to speak in the church" (1 Corinthians 14:35, *New International Version*) as well as this: "wives should submit to their husbands in everything." (Ephesians 5:24) But the Christian woman has a consolation prize: "women will be saved through childbearing—if they continue in faith, love and holiness with propriety." (1 Timothy 2:15) Apparently, all the Christian women who died in childbirth over the past nineteen centuries must have been faithless, hateful, and unholy.

As usual, Paul's focus is on his twin obsessions, submission and sex, or specifically avoiding sex: "you should avoid sexual immorality; that each of you should learn to control your own body…The Lord will punish all those who commit such sins." (1 Thessalonians 4:3, 6) Paul, the congregation's daddy who has arranged its marriage, is primarily concerned with wifely chastity: "I promised you to one husband, to Christ, so that I might present you as a pure virgin to him." (1 Corinthians 11:2) The church is Jesus' bride, cleansed "by the washing with water through the word…without stain or wrinkle or any other blemish, but holy and blameless." (Ephesians 5: 26-27) Little wonder that their obsession with sexual purity led some in the early church to castrate themselves and the later church to require vows of celibacy for priests and nuns. Thanks to Christianity, millions of people even in the twenty-first century believe virgins are "defiled" by sex. "These are those who did not defile themselves with women, for they remained virgins. They follow the Lamb wherever he goes."

(Revelation 14:4) The divorced are second-hand goods, their status defined by sexual purity: "Everyone who divorces his wife and marries another commits adultery, and he who marries a woman divorced from her husband commits adultery." (Luke 16:18)

Paul clearly accepted Rome's system of chattel slavery as basic to the human condition. In fact, merely to be human is to be a slave: "[Jesus] emptied himself, taking *the form of a slave* (*morphēn doulou*), coming in human likeness; and found human in appearance." (Philippians 2:7, *New American Bible*) "To be human, therefore, is to be a slave... Slavery exists as a normal state of existence for human beings...Paul understands slavery to be an inherent aspect of life as a human being."[82] Christian discipleship is slavery: "Don't you know that when you offer yourselves to someone as obedient slaves, you are slaves of the one you obey— whether you are slaves to sin, which leads to death, or to obedience, which leads to righteousness?...though you used to be slaves to sin, you have come to obey from your heart the pattern of teaching that has now claimed your allegiance. You have been set free from sin and have become slaves to righteousness. I am using an example from everyday life...Just as you used to offer yourselves as slaves to impurity and to ever-increasing wickedness, so now offer yourselves as slaves to righteousness leading to holiness. When you were slaves to sin, you were free from the control of righteousness...But now that you have been set free from sin and have become slaves of God." (Romans 6:16-20, 22) Freedom is slavery, and slavery freedom. If I were to tell you going around raping people is freedom and being a decent chap is slavery, you might think me a candidate for psychiatric intervention.

Why would we expect that a man who believed *to be born human is slavery by definition* would object to slavery? "Were you a slave when you were called? Don't let it trouble you—although if you can gain your freedom, do so…the one who was free when called is Christ's slave…each person, as responsible to God, should remain in the situation they were in when God called them." (1 Corinthians 7:21, 24) *For Paul, slavery, whether physical or spiritual, is the natural state of humanity.* "It is for freedom that Christ has set us free" (Galatians 5:1) means "you have been set free from sin and have become slaves to righteousness." (Romans 6:18) For Paul, *freedom means obedience to a different master.* A "Hebrew of Hebrews" (Philippians 3:5), Paul was trained in the law of Moses that stipulated a male slave would go free after seven years but his wife and children remained the property of his former master: "the woman and her children shall belong to her master, and only the man shall go free." (Exodus 21:4) By virtue of both his Jewish religious and Roman social acculturation, Paul has literally no understanding of freedom that approximates our own.

The freedom Paul imagines isn't an autonomous "personal relationship" with Jesus, much less freedom in the abstract. God works through a hierarchy "appointed for the church: first are apostles, second are prophets, third are teachers, then those who do miracles, those who have the gift of healing, those who can help others, those who have the gift of leadership, those who speak in unknown languages." (1 Corinthians 12:28, *New Living Translation*) "Obey your leaders and submit to their authority." (Hebrews 13:17) Obedience to leaders was obviously an expectation from Christianity's beginning: "Therefore, my dear friends, as you have always obeyed—not only in my presence, but now much more in my absence—continue to work out your salvation with fear and trembling." (Philippians 2:12) Submit to authority, obey with fear and trembling.

The forgers claiming to write in Paul's name accepted slavery as well: "Slaves, obey your earthly masters with respect and fear, and with sincerity of heart, just as you would obey Christ...Serve wholeheartedly, as if you were serving the Lord." (Ephesians 6:5, 7) Indeed, early Christians endorsed slavery without reservation according to Christianity's founding documents: "Slaves, obey your earthly masters in everything; and do it, not only when their eye is on you and to curry their favor, but with sincerity of heart and reverence for the Lord." (Colossians 3:22) "You who are slaves must accept the authority of your masters with all respect. Do what they tell you—not only if they are kind and reasonable, but even if they are cruel." (1 Peter 2:18) Only within the last few decades have scholars pushed back on this issue, particularly historian Keith Bradley, who has specialized in early Christianity's stance on slavery.[83] "Bradley aimed to explode the myth, born of the nineteenth-century abolitionist era, that held up Stoic philosophy and (especially) ancient Christianity as the two main agents of change that ameliorated, and eventually ended, Roman slavery…[Bradley's writing] challenges the historiography of progress as anachronistic and wholly inappropriate for understanding slavery in Rome."[84]

Slaves in Rome were typically deracinated trophies of war, born of slave parents, or paupers who sold themselves into servitude to escape starvation. They could be freely beaten and tortured, executed by crucifixion if they attempted to escape, sold at the whim of their owners, and were frequent objects of sexual exploitation; "slaves had almost no rights at all and were de facto prostitutes peopling the houses of the free."[85] Most prostitutes, both women and children, were slaves—"women and children were always considered property…the *doulos* [slave] is an owned person."[86] "Roman law declared the slave clearly to be property, essentially no different than a farm implement or domesticated animal…"[87] "Slaves were treated like objects; they had no rights; they did not even possess the right to life…Certain fundamental principles of slavery applied to all slaves in the ancient world, namely the *dominus* possessed the slave, including his/her life, workforce, and property. Therefore, slavery meant to be unfree."[88] Sexual exploitation of people in servitude, men, women, and children, was a ubiquitous reality of slavery and it is impossible that early Christians, obsessed with sexual purity, were unaware of it. "Christianity was born and grew up in a world in which slaveholders and slaves were part of the everyday landscape. In a context in which slaveholders treated slaves as bodies— available bodies, vulnerable bodies, compliant bodies, surrogate bodies—ascetic Christians learned to treat their own bodies as slaves."[89]

A recent reevaluation of early Christianity's attitude toward slavery concludes, "Christianity brought about little or no change for slaves. And in place of the love that Christianity advocated, oftentimes the writings of the early fathers of the Church contain words of disdain or even hatred." The *Didache*, a Christian pastoral work composed in the early second century, taught that slave masters were a stand-in for God. "When [slaves] are in the presence of the master, they are to consider themselves in the physical presence of God. When they look at the master, they are to think of God."[90]

A rational person might expect the calm acceptance of human trafficking and the sexual exploitation of women and children would utterly disqualify the Bible as a source of moral authority—a bit of research reveals a flurry of recent books and articles on slavery in the literature of New Testament studies, evidence of the embarrassment this issue still causes in academic circles. However, it is also possible for believers to simply dismiss the egregious moral failings of the "God-breathed" scriptures, a recent case in point being *Inspired Imperfection*, an apologetic book by Gregory A. Boyd. Boyd unironically claims, "the Bible's so-called 'problems' are not genuine problems that need to be solved; they actually *contribute to* [emphasis in original] the inspired authority and central message of Scripture...this ancient collection of writings contains a multitude of errors, contradictions, and historical inaccuracies, as well as a good bit of morally offensive material..."[91] Despite the claim that it marked the dawn of a new age of ethics in human relations—"love your neighbor as yourself"—in Christianity, as in any other cult, *religion prevails over morality.* "Ethical statements based on ethical elements of Biblical texts do not build upon an argumentative justification based on reason, but on a 'theological justification.' 'Theological justifications'—by their nature—refer to transcendence and thus provoke the suspicion that they delude further rational inquiry and arguments that would lead to proofs and conclusions."[92] The conclusion a person might very well make is that the New Testament has no moral relevance whatsoever based on a rational examination of its text.

Part 5: FACT EXEMPT, TAX EXEMPT, ABOVE THE LAW

FACT EXEMPT

"It is certain because it is impossible."

Tertullian

"Faith is to believe what you do not see. The reward of this faith is to see what you believe."

Augustine of Hippo

"Sacrifice the intellect to God."

Ignatius of Loyola

"Reason is the Devil's greatest whore."

Martin Luther

Belief, particularly blind belief, is a blessing: "Blessed are those who have not seen and yet have believed." (John 20:29) "Now faith is confidence in what we hope for and assurance about what we do not see. This is what the ancients were commended for." (Hebrews 11:1-2) Believers "live by faith, not by sight." (2 Corinthians 5:7) "The righteous will live by faith." (Romans 1:17) Consistent with his focus on belief, Paul keeps things small and keeps things tidy: "If you declare with your mouth, 'Jesus is Lord,' and believe in your heart that God raised him from the dead, you will be saved." (Romans 10:9) Christian epistemology is simple: hearing is believing—"faith comes from hearing the message, and the message is heard through the word about Christ" (Romans

10:17)—which goes some way toward explaining the Christian obsession with preaching as well as the accusations that rival preachers are false prophets and minions of Satan. If you believe it, it's real.

Bible stories are also a source of belief—"written that you may believe that Jesus is the Messiah, the Son of God" (John 20:31)—and *the stories are their own confirmation*. In short, the *soi-disant* evidence of the gospels is hearsay at best, anonymous secondhand confections written by people who didn't see what (if anything) really happened. To no one's surprise, modern Christian apologists, armed with stacks of diplomas from Bible colleges, have ginned up books and blogs by the hundreds to validate the conflicting, nonsensical New Testament stories, The very fact that Bible stories require a small army of trained apologists to Jesusplain the contradictions is *prima facie* evidence the stories are fabrications. When something makes sense, we don't have to invent reasons to believe it, but given skepticism about Bible stories generally, dozens of Bible colleges now offer degrees in apologetics such as Regent University's "Apologetics and Cosmogony," an online course of study that prepares non-scientists to defend Bronze Age creation myths.

The apologist may respond by quoting Acts 1:3: "[Jesus] presented himself to them *and gave many convincing proofs* that he was alive. He appeared to them over a period of forty days and spoke about the kingdom of God." Given what the

68

first installment of Luke/Acts says, the "proofs" were likely passages from the Old Testament that Christians believed foretold a messiah who shows up after centuries of expectation only to be arrested and executed—"beginning with Moses and all the Prophets, he explained to them what was said in all the Scriptures concerning himself." (Luke 24:27) When Paul tried a similar tactic in court, it didn't go well: "'I am saying nothing beyond what the prophets and Moses said would happen—that the Messiah would suffer and, as the first to rise from the dead, would bring the message of light to his own people and to the Gentiles.'" At this point Porcius Festus, the procurator of Judea, interrupted Paul's defense. "'You are out of your mind, Paul!'" he shouted. "'*Your many scriptures (ta polla se grammata)* are driving you insane.'" (Acts 26:22-24) Readers interested in how New Testament figures like Paul mangled and misapplied scriptures are directed to Robert Miller's comprehensive discussion.[93]

The writer's claim that Jesus was "the first to rise from the dead" is confusing. He has already recounted the resurrection of the son of the widow on Nain—"The dead man sat up and began to talk, and Jesus gave him back to his mother" (Luke 7:15)—as well as the raising of Jairus' daughter: "They laughed at [Jesus], knowing that she was dead. But he took her by the hand and said, 'My child, get up!' Her spirit returned, and at once she stood up." (Luke 8:53-55) The author of Luke/Acts evidently can't decide who was really "the first to rise from the dead." So how did he know (or not)?

Let's have Paul remind us how Christians know things: "This is what we speak, not in words taught us by human wisdom but in words taught by the Spirit, explaining spiritual realities with Spirit-taught words. The person without the Spirit does not accept the things that come from the Spirit of God but considers them foolishness and cannot understand them because they are discerned only through the Spirit. The person with the Spirit makes judgments about all things, but such a person is not subject to merely human judgments...we have the mind of Christ." (1 Corinthians 2:13-16) Since a "person with the Spirit makes judgments about all things" it should come as no surprise to hear "Spirit-taught" preachers sermonizing about evolutionary biology, geology, cosmology, natural history, medicine, sexology, virology, and various other fields in which they have zero expertise—if you think you know something, then you do!

In the considered opinion of oft-quoted evangelical philosopher extraordinaire, William Lane Craig, "The way in which I know Christianity is true is first and foremost on the basis of the witness of the Holy Spirit in my heart. And this gives me self-authenticating means of knowing Christianity is true wholly apart from the evidence." What is a "self-authenticating means of knowing...wholly apart from the evidence" but *belief in belief* and how would we distinguish belief in belief from, say, mental illness?

"Now about the gifts of the Spirit, brothers, I do not want you to be uninformed...To one there is given through the Spirit a message of wisdom, to another *a message of knowledge* by means of the same Spirit, to another faith by the same Spirit, to another gifts of healing by that one Spirit, to another miraculous powers, to another prophecy, to another distinguishing between spirits, to another speaking in different kinds of tongues, and to still another the interpretation of tongues." (1 Corinthians 12:1, 8-10) Put in context—apologists are always clamoring for *more context*—Spirit-acquired "knowledge" must be as real as medically verifiable "gifts of healing," cell phone videos documenting "miraculous powers" of wonder-working Christians, and all that fulfilled prophecy, to say nothing (pun intended) of those "different kinds of tongues" that Paul admitted were incomprehensible.

No one really knows exactly how the "gifts of the Spirit" scam worked in the first century, but an ex-evangelical panjandrum tells how it works in the present. Regarding "leaders of the religious right" he met in person, Frank Schaeffer said, "In private they ranged from unreconstructed bigot reactionaries like Jerry Falwell, to Dr. Dobson, the most power-hungry and ambitious person I have ever met, to Billy Graham, a very weird man indeed who lived an oddly sheltered life in a celebrity/ministry cocoon, to Pat

Robertson, who would have a hard time finding work in any job where hearing voices is not a requirement...On the [700] *Club* that day there was an interesting moment. The floor director was doing what floor directors do everywhere, silently counting down on her fat fingers so Pat could wrap things up for the break. Pat was having a Word of Knowledge. That's when God tells Pat things directly, as if he's on the phone calling in information about, say, some woman in Milwaukee with a tumor in her left ovary...[the floor director] was counting down the seconds on her fingers to the out. And Pat wrapped up the Word of Knowledge right on cue! Since a Word of Knowledge is as direct a message from God as you can get this side of the Last Judgment, it interested me to learn that God made sure his Word fit the time slot."[94]

Of course, no one ever claimed that taking advice from spirits is without its problems. "The Spirit clearly says that in later times some will abandon the faith and follow deceiving spirits and things taught by demons." (1 Timothy 4:1) Given the explosion of "false prophets" and "things taught by demons," in the early churches, by the end of the first century Christian enthusiasm for listening to spirts began to cool a bit, but the Real Christians™ hit upon an ingenious solution: "Beloved, do not believe every spirit, but test the spirits to see whether they are from God, for many false prophets have gone out into the world...Whoever knows God listens to us; whoever is not

72

from God does not listen to us. By this we know the Spirit of truth and the spirit of error." (1 John 4:1, 6) If they listen, they know God and you're right, but if they don't listen, then, "the god of this age has blinded the minds of unbelievers." (2 Corinthians 4:4) Problem solved! Whatever happens, the Real Christians™ are speaking truth and we know that because someone's listening to them!

"Truly I tell you, unless you change and become like little children, you will never enter the kingdom of heaven." (Matthew 18:3) Like little children, the heroes of the New Testament believe what they're told and have an imaginary friend—C.S. Lewis, a revered Christian apologist, was also a prolific writer of children's fantasy stories which makes perfect sense if you think about it.

"The Spirit told Philip, 'Go to that chariot and stay near it'...While Peter was still thinking about the vision, the Spirit said to him, 'Simon, three men are looking for you'...the Holy Spirit said, 'Set apart for me Barnabas and Saul for the work to which I have called them'...The Holy Spirit says, 'In this way the Jewish leaders in Jerusalem will bind the owner of this belt and will hand him over to the Gentiles.'" (Acts 8:29, 10:19, 13:2, 21:11) In a world that swarmed with oracles, mediums, shamans, and prophets, the early Christians were just the latest to claim they spoke with spirits.

Christianity's Roman critics charged "both the believers and the scriptures they read and trusted lacked intellectual integrity...followers of Jesus were ridiculed as ignorant, gullible fools, and for mainly consisting of women and fanatics."[95] Paul's house churches "can be characterized as a spirit-possession cult. Paul establishes communities of those possessed by the spirit of Jesus."[96] "The worshippers and the attending spirits form a double assembly"[97] which Paul himself acknowledges: "because you are *zealous devotees of spirits*" (*zēlōtai este pneumatōv*). (1 Corinthians 14:3) Paul says of the jabbering Christian, "no one understands him; he utters mysteries with his spirit" and concedes that an unbeliever entering a house church full of raving Christians would encounter a pandemonium of the spirit-possessed— "if the whole church comes together and all speak in tongues and strangers or unbelievers enter, will they not say you are possessed?" (1 Corinthians 14:2, 23) What would unbelievers have thought of Paul's own incomprehensible speech? Very likely what the Roman historian Livy thought of the spirit-possessed followers of Dionysus: "Men, as if their minds had been taken from them, prophesied with frenzied tossings of their bodies."[98] Those who understand some basics of evolution know the human brain is a patchwork of adaptations, not specifically wired to process either logic or probability, and not designed to distinguish between rational discourse and gibberish. Our nearest living relatives are chimps; those who are unaware of the implications of our family tree are also blissfully unaware we can produce a wondrously modulated string of monkey sounds we mistake for revelations by spirits.

In a chilling declaration, Paul sets out the roadmap to Christian totalitarianism: "We demolish arguments and every pretension that sets itself up against the knowledge of God, and we take captive every thought to make it obedient to Christ. And we will be ready to punish every act of disobedience, once your obedience is complete." (2 Corinthians 10:5-6) For Paul, the accumulated wisdom of his age is foolishness: "If any of you think you are wise by the standards of this age, you should become fools so that you may become wise. For the wisdom of this world is foolishness in God's sight." (1 Corinthians 3:18-19) By the fourth century, as Christianity took control of society, "for many hardline Christian clerics, the entire edifice of academic learning was considered dubious. In some ways there was a noble egalitarianism in this...But there was a more aggressive and sinister side to it, too. St. Paul had succinctly and influentially said that 'the wisdom of this world is foolishness with God.' This was an attitude that persisted...Intellectual simplicity or, to put a less flattering name on it, ignorance was widely celebrated...Ignorance was power."[99] Become like little children. Become fools. As the "fathers of the church" were aware, little children have imaginary friends, believe whatever they're told, and have virtually no logical skills, hence the modern Christian enthusiasm for banning books, particularly books for children lest they begin to think.

A grand system exists that reflects ancient humanity's abysmal primordial ignorance about basically everything in the natural world while including every bias and logical fallacy known or yet to be discovered. We call this grand system *religion*. Some ancient people, called the Jews, believed their god required the blood sacrifice of inordinate numbers of animals, while other ancient people, called the Aztecs, believed gods required the blood sacrifice of inordinate numbers of humans, yet others, called the Christians, believed god shed his own blood as a human sacrifice, and others, called the Catholics, believed they must regularly eat some of god's body and drink his blood. All this before H.P. Lovecraft wrote a single story!

To regard the triumph of Christianity as merely the victory of one religion over others is to completely miss the significance of the new intellectual regime that would dominate the Western world for the next fifteen centuries. Far more than a set of doctrines, Christianity became the framework around which an enduring social order arose, a distorting prism through which a culture viewed the natural world, and a totalitarian ethos that sought out and destroyed all that challenged it. A poignant example is the attempted rescue of the *Archimedes Codex*, a collection of works by the greatest mathematical genius of the pre-Christian era. A monk scraped the original writing off the parchment on which it had been copied, cut the pages into pieces, and used the vandalized result to create a prayer book. "The first piece of parchment in [the Christian scribe's] new codex contained *On Floating Bodies*. He covered it with a blessing of loaves for Easter. Further into the codex, he wrote over a different section with a prayer for repentance."[100] *On Floating Bodies* is the first known work on hydrostatics, what causes some objects to float and others to sink.

The New Testament records the first example of Christian book burning: "a number of those who had practiced magic arts brought their books together and burned them in the sight of all." (Acts 19:19, *English Standard Version*) "The burning of books was part of the advent and imposition of Christianity."[101] The Council of Ephesus (431 CE) decreed the philosopher Porphyry's books be burned and the Christian emperor Justinian (529 CE) ordered books deemed anti-Christian be burned as well. Julian's *Against the Christians* survives only in the form of partial quotations in a refutation written by Cyril of Alexandria, the cleric infamous for inciting a Christian mob that murdered and dismembered Hypatia, the Alexandrian mathematician and philosopher.

TAX EXEMPT

Ever since the Roman emperor Constantine decided Christianity was a good investment, monetary policy put the Church in the lap of luxury. "Tax relief was given to Christian lands, clerics were exempted from public duties, bishops were lavished with gifts and banquets, annual allowances were given to widows, virgins, and nuns."[102] The estimated 380,000 churches in the US—nearly 250,000 more churches than there are K-12 schools—are exempt from federal, state, and local taxes, including property taxes, regardless of income. Churches are also exempt from sales taxes and capital gains taxes on investments. Donations to churches are tax deductible. Communities dependent on property taxes to fund police and fire departments can't count on sprawling mega-churches to pay for their own protection. If you're living in such a community, you're contributing to those churches, paying the freight, like it or not.

Churches even evade basic requirements of fiscal transparency. Churches have been exempted from financial disclosure since 1943 based on the assumption that they're in business to do "the Lord's work." Religious "non-profits" aren't churches—they don't have pews or congregations— but they have successfully requested that they be reclassified as churches and in many cases the IRS has complied. The Billy Graham Evangelistic Association is a "church." So is Gideons International, the group that plants Bibles in motel rooms. Focus On The Family, a virulently homophobic outfit based in Colorado Springs, is a "church" that advocates "conversion therapy" based on junk psychology. "While reasons for this growing trend vary, these groups may share one main goal: keeping their donor lists private to protect their donors from public criticism or backlash...some of these donors can deduct their donations from their taxable income through the charitable deduction, creating an incentive to support those groups."[103] As tax law currently stands, religious reactionaries can anonymously damage the lives of people they will never have to confront and claim a tax deduction in the process.

According to analysis reported by the *Washington Post*, total subsidies of religion have been guesstimated at $71 billion, but the report concluded, "That's almost certainly a lowball, as they didn't estimate the cost of a number of subsidies, like local income and property tax exemptions, the sales tax exemption and—most importantly—charitable deduction...Their estimate that religious groups own $600 billion in property is also probably low, since it leaves out property besides actual churches, mosques, etc."[104]

As Paul says, "the Lord has commanded that those who preach the gospel should receive their living from the gospel." (1 Corinthians 9:14) Although the average annual income for ministers is around $50,000, for some it can be substantially higher. As of 2022, Kenneth Copeland's net worth was estimated to be $300 million, celebrity preacher Joel Osteen's net worth was thought to be $100 million, and televangelist Creflo Dollar's was pegged at $26 million. But Joyce Meyer and Paula White scored a paltry $8 million and $5 million respectively which seems fitting—according to Paul, women shouldn't be talking in church in the first place.

God is good for some, even better for others. As Posner noted, despite revelations of "their flamboyance, secrecy about money, and apocalyptic world view…lavish spending, or bizarre policy prescriptions,"[105] to say nothing of continuous exposés of questionable finances, sexual scandal, and outlandish pronouncements, the carny world of Christian evangelism continues to be a multibillion-dollar enterprise.

Religious exceptionalism has real world consequences. Ryan Cragun, a Florida professor, examined the effect of church tax avoidance on Manatee County, Florida, "a fairly representative illustration of the nation generally" due to its mix of urban and rural areas. Cragun concluded, "By downloading the 'just market values' for the 360 properties classified as having a religious exemption, I was able to work out that their combined value was $406.7 million. If they paid the standard property taxes required of both commercial and residential properties in Manatee County, they would add $8.5 million to the tax revenue of the county annually. With the county's budget at $740 million, an additional $8.5 million works out to be about 1.1% of the total. This, according to the 2022 Manatee Country budget proposal, would be enough to cover the building of all three newly proposed emergency medical services stations in the county, along with upgrades of EMS equipment and its 911 service." Extrapolating from the case of Manatee County, Cragun estimated "local and state governments forgo roughly $6.9 billion in tax revenue annually by exempting religions from paying property taxes."[106] In a nation beset by homelessness and under-funded social services, why are taxpayers subsidizing Joel Osteen's $10.5 million Houston "parsonage" or Kenneth Copeland's Fort Worth airport and his three private jets?

ABOVE THE LAW

"There is no crime for those who have Christ."

Saint Shenoute the Archimandrite

"With or without religion, good people can behave well and bad people can do evil; but for good people to do evil—that takes religion."

Steven Weinberg

For the mere sake of space, we will skip Christianity's support of wars since before the Crusades. It was Constantine I, fighting his co-emperor Maxentius, who saw a cross of light and above it, *in hoc signo vinces, in this sign shalt thou conquer.* After the vision of 312 CE, Constantine used the *chi rho* sign on his military standards and Christians have been "marching as to war with the cross of Jesus going on before" ever since. Neither will I trouble the reader with Christianity's dalliance with dictators—from the twentieth century onward, the alliance between Christianity and fascism has been the most enduring and most devoted same sex marriage in history.

81

Nor will we retrace the dusty timeworn paths of the witch trials, the torture and burning of heretics and dissenters, the homicidal internecine spats between Christian sects, the genocide of colonized peoples, or Christendom's centuries-long enthusiasm for the slave trade. All these horrors, we're assured, were primarily the result of unenlightened and superstitious minds acting in an ignorant age. Instead, I propose we lower the moral bar to the dirt and cast aside every ethical standard but the most primordial: the treatment of children.

Under most circumstances adults will do anything to protect children. Bystanders will enter burning houses, throw themselves into a raging torrent or donate an organ to save a child. Infantile facial features capture our attention and elicit protective responses and caregiving—there's even a term of art for it, *Kindchenschema*. Society is organized to protect children. Communities have child protective services, and many professions require licensees to report even the suspicion of child abuse to state authorities. Here in the US, medical specialists and subspecialists labor in 250 hospitals dedicated to the treatment of children.

Not only human children but the young of other species, notably puppies and kittens, evoke positive emotional responses as advertisers are abundantly aware. Like other mammals, humans have evolved a basic instinct to protect the young; they are biologically preconditioned to protect their offspring. Videos of humans rescuing baby kangaroos, otters, whales, elephants, rhinos, foxes, squirrels, and chimps are viewed by millions of people. Protection of the young is the definition of love.

Jesus, the nominal founder of Christianity, put his disciples on notice: "'whoever welcomes one such child in my name welcomes me. If anyone causes one of these little ones—those who believe in me—to stumble, it would be better for them to have a large millstone hung around their neck and to be drowned in the depths of the sea.'" (Matthew 18:5-6) Even if Gospel Jesus was only talking about "those who believe in me" and only comparing them to real children, one might expect that abusing literal children would be unacceptable if only by implication. Obviously indigenous peoples murdered by Christian *génocidaires* and missionaries, Jews, Muslims, and "heretics" murdered by Christians during the Middle Ages, the victims of Christian slave traders, and Christians murdered by fellow Christians over sectarian disputes up to modern times *were likely parents of dependent children*, but leaving those considerations aside, let's focus instead on the fate of children *under the direct influence and care of Christian churches*.

The general public became aware of sexual molestation of children in the archdiocese of Boston in 2002 when a team of investigative reporters published a series of exposés in *The Boston Globe*. The series of reports won the Pulitzer Prize in 2003 and the investigation was dramatized in the film *Spotlight* which won two Academy Awards in 2016. The reporters, who initially thought they were dealing with a single priest who had sexually assaulted young boys, soon discovered scores of priests were implicated and that the Catholic hierarchy had transferred clerics to unsuspecting parishes, intimidated victims and their families, and failed to report sexual assault of children to authorities despite knowing of cases of serial sexual abuse for years.[107] In response to a tsunami of lawsuits, the Boston archdiocese closed seventy parishes and the archbishop, Cardinal Bernard Law, resigned his position. Cardinal Law had known for at least two decades about rampant sexual crimes committed by clergy, including the infamous case of John Geoghan, a priest who raped or molested over 130 children in six parishes over a period of thirty years. Relieved of his duties, Law absquatulated to the Vatican where Pope John Paul II—who was declared a saint in 2013—appointed him Archpriest of the Basilica of Santa Maria Maggiore with a salary of $12,000 a month.

Any hope that the Boston diocese was an outlier, an isolated case of off-the-rails atrocity, was soon quashed. Reports of serial sexual abuse of children by priests exploded across the US and the world. Bishop Accountability.org maintains an online database of "Publicly Accused Roman Catholic Priests, Nuns, Brothers, Deacons, and Seminarians" searchable by "diocese, religious order, state, or alphabetical." In short, rampant criminality in America's largest denomination compelled the creation of a website that "provides convenient access, for law enforcement and other interested persons, to the names of all US Catholic clergy accused of sexually abusing children and/or possessing child abuse images, commonly referred to as child pornography."[108]

Anyone expecting the Church would concentrate on meaningful acts of contrition, like the "penance and prayer" commonly prescribed for priests suspended due to a credible accusations of raping children, was in for a rude awakening. A news report in 2019 revealed the Church spent $10.6 million lobbying in various states "to fight legislation that would help victims of clergy sexual abuse seek justice" including New York's Child Victims Act that extended the statute of limitations that increased the age limit at which victims are able to sue.[109] The motive for lobbying against victim compensation is clear—the Church is protecting its finances. It is estimated the Catholic Church has paid out $4 billion to settle at least 8,600 suits brought by victims of clergy abuse.

By this point, most would think the situation could get no worse, but even more deplorable news was soon to be revealed from the storied "isle of saints and scholars," Catholic Ireland. After nine years of hearing evidence the Commission to Inquire into Child Abuse (CICA) released a five-volume, 3000-page report "of sadistic physical, sexual, emotional abuse, neglect and brutalization of children in

Ireland's industrial school system...*which will not lead to the prosecution of those individually or collectively guilty of crimes against thousands of children* (emphasis added). Neither has political responsibility been attributed. "The report by Judge Sean Ryan continues to obscure the role of the Catholic Church, which is an essential element of the Irish state, and successive governments in operating a cruel workhouse system which at least 170,000 children passed through in the middle decades of the twentieth century...All the staff carried leather straps which were freely used on children. A Brother Oliver repeatedly beat children with particular violence. One victim reported, 'I was running trying to get away from him. He hit me, it didn't matter where, legs, back, head, anywhere.' Oliver forced one 12-year-old child to lick excrement from his shoes...Sexual abuse was rife. Artane's staff hosted a number of Brothers who had repeatedly been warned for 'embracing and fondling' boys. Two such paedophiles went on to be hung for child murder in Canada. Others accused of rape, beat or bribed their victims into silence. Accused Brothers were invariably excused, lightly admonished or, typically, moved to other institutions where they were free to continue abusing children for decades."[110]

As usual, the Church concealed or destroyed evidence and suborned authorities to protect its reputation as a moral paragon, but particularly to protect its purse. "The Catholic religious orders that ran more than 50 workhouse-style reform schools from the late 19th century until the mid-1990's offered public words of apology, shame and regret Wednesday. But when questioned, their leaders indicated they would continue to protect the identities of clergy accused of abuse, men and women who were never reported to police, and were instead permitted to change jobs and keep harming children. The Christian Brothers... successfully sued the commission in 2004 to keep the identities of all its members, dead or alive, unnamed in the report. No names, whether of victims or perpetrators, appear in the final document." Survivors of decades of horror were paid $90,000 each "on condition they surrender their right to sue either the church or the state."[111]

The Church orders that ran the schools avoided accountability and remained above the law. "Sexual rape after corporal punishment, of [which] flogging was the norm, practiced by most of the sadist Oblates that ran the school. Later it transpired that one of the worst Brothers in the Industrial School had a conviction for raping young boys in Wales. The school and the Oblates knew this but did nothing. In the 17 years that the Brother was working in St. Conleth's, Daingean, he raped and flogged hundreds of more boys. A few boys died at his hands."[112]

Wherever Catholic religious orders went, the touch of evil followed. In 2014 a local historian, Catherine Corless, discovered the unmarked graves of 700 children on the grounds of Saint Mary's Mother and Baby Home, the Tuam workhouse for unwed mothers run by a Catholic order, the Sisters of Bon Secours, named, without irony, in honor of Notre Dame de Bonsecours, Our Lady of Comfort. In 2017 a survey using ground penetrating radar conducted by Irish police confirmed the presence of hundreds of children's bodies in a disused septic tank. The Bon Secours order claimed the underground structure was a 'burial chamber,' but further investigation quickly confirmed the bodies had been discarded like sewage. Of the 3,251 babies that passed through the Tuam workhouse, 802 are known from death certificates to have perished, an infant mortality rate of 25%. Many who survived were raffled off by the nuns to American Catholics who chose children based on photos, mail order children sold to parents of unknown qualifications. After adoption, some of those children were sexually abused.

An eventual investigation into the state-financed, church-run mother and baby homes found that some 9,000 children had died in the care of religious orders such as the Sisters of the Sacred Hearts of Jesus and Mary. Representatives of the various orders offered strategic apologies and promises of cooperation after the truth came out while maneuvering to avoid legal and financial repercussions for decades of cruelty and neglect. Rather than investigating the carnage as suspicious deaths, the Irish Republic dithered for years before proposing a special law that may permit exhumation and forensic examination of children's remains. "The result is that there will be no finding of blame or responsibility in law for their deaths," Kevin Higgins said. "The rationale seems to be that, as these children clearly had no rights while alive, why embarrass ourselves by giving them any rights in death?"[113]

The horrors of state-supported, church-run gulags for children didn't end in Ireland. "Unmarked graves that may hold the bodies of more than 160 Indigenous children were found this month on Penelakut Island...In addition to the Penelakut Island graves, unmarked burials at three more locations were detected by First Nations communities between May and July using ground-penetrating radar scans...remains of 215 children were buried at the former Kamloops Indian Residential School, run by the Catholic Church in British Columbia from 1890 until 1978...Just a few weeks later, on June 24, the Cowessess First Nation announced that radar scans detected up to 751 unmarked graves at the site of the Marieval Indian Residential School in Saskatchewan, operated by the Catholic Church from 1899 to 1997. Then, on June 30, representatives of the Lower Kootenay Band, a member band of the Krunaxa Nation, revealed that a recent search at the site of the former St. Eugene's Mission School—another Catholic institution in British Columbia, open from 1890 to 1970—uncovered another 182 unmarked, shallow graves holding children's remains...Until 1951, all Indigenous children ages 7 to 15 were required by law to attend a residential school...The 2015 report by the Truth and Reconciliation Commission documented 3,200 children who died while at residential schools, but the number of deaths could be 10 times higher than that…many of the children's families were never notified about their deaths."[114]

Residential schools were also common in the United States; thousands of children disappeared into a genocidal hell where speaking their native languages was forbidden, brutal punishments were meted out, and sexual molestation of boys and girls was common. There were at least 408 schools operating in 37 American states and territories from 1819 to 1969.[115] Over 150 such church-run "schools" existed in Canada. Besides the Catholic Church, Methodists, Presbyterians, and Episcopalian churches ran boarding schools expressly dedicated to the eradication of Indigenous culture and language. Additional revelations of government-sponsored race hatred and child abuse at hundreds of church-administered reeducation camps will inevitably emerge. And church officials will follow a predictable script: express their shame and sorrow and promise to uncover the truth about the children's lives Christian orders so carefully deleted and the bodies they so casually buried while avoiding a legal and financial judgment day.

Following the exposure of child molestation and rape in Catholic parishes, those of us who follow the grotesquerie of churches calmly marked our calendar and waited for the Protestant shoe to drop. It was not long in coming. In 2019, a team of investigative reporters at the *Houston Chronicle* published a six-part exposé, "Abuse of Faith," that laid out in detail the efforts of the Executive Committee of the Southern Baptist Convention to conceal evidence and evade the legal consequences of sexual predation in affiliated churches. "The men who controlled the Executive Committee (EC)—which runs day-to-day operations of the Southern Baptist Convention (SBC)—knew the scope of the problem. But working closely with their lawyers, they maligned the people who wanted to do something about abuse and repeatedly rejected pleas for help and reform... Almost always, the internal focus was on protecting the SBC from legal liability and not caring for survivors or creating any plan to prevent sexual abuse within SBC churches."[116]

Once the floodgates opened, a tsunami of accusations burst forth. Several women accused evangelical apologetics guru and celebrity author, Ravi Zacharias, of sexual assault. A report produced after *Christianity Today* published news of the accusations says, "Eight therapists reported that Mr. Zacharias would start the message either completely nude or would remove the sheets during the message. Six therapists reported that he always or almost always had an erection during the message."[117] A previously secret list of accused sex abusers, released due to public pressure by the Southern Baptist Convention, runs to 205 pages and is guaranteed to be incomplete.

For generations—and likely for centuries—Christian churches have been a hunting ground for sexual predators and psychopaths. Churches have historically chosen immunity over accountability and secrecy over disclosure, creating a culture in which adults were free to abuse children with impunity. In all areas, intellectual, financial, and ethical, the goal of the church is to operate without restraint, above the law. But in the instant information age there has been a price to pay for churches. Will Americans abandoning churches ever reconnect, and if not, why not? "First, for a variety of reasons, churches do not enjoy the same status and public confidence they once had...trust and confidence in organized religion have plummeted over the past two decades" and a clear majority of the unaffiliated "disagree that children should be raised in a religious community."[118] Logically we might expect distrust of churches to deepen as reports of children "disciplined" to death, trafficked, sexually assaulted, and effectively murdered by preachers performing "exorcisms" continue to appear in the news. Paul was unsparing in his invective against 'pagans' who "abandoned natural relations with women and were inflamed with lust for one another. Men committed shameful acts with other men" and Paul was certain "those who do such things deserve death." (Romans 1: 27, 32) Paul said nothing about what Christian ministers who rape children deserve. I suppose we'll have to "judge nothing before the appointed time; wait until the Lord comes" (1 Corinthians 4:5) to figure that part out, but Gospel Jesus may have offered a clue: the pastors who failed to gouge out an eye or cut off a hand to

92

keep from sinning, who have betrayed "the church of God, which he bought with his own blood" (Acts 20:28), are apparently destined "to be thrown into hell." (Matthew 5:29) If only.

Part 6: THE SKEPTIC'S *PANARION*

Epiphanius (d. 403), the bishop of Salamis on the island of Cyprus, wrote a lengthy treatise called the *Panarion* that refuted eighty "heresies," sixty of which covered the beliefs of dissident Christian splinter groups the bishop considered heterodox. The title of Epiphanius' safe sects manual, derived from the Latin *panarium, breadbasket,* is a self-described "chest of remedies for those whom savage beasts have bitten."[119] In this section, I offer my own medicine cabinet of remedies against the hydrophobia of belief in belief.

It has often been observed that every person finds the Jesus he's looking for. Indeed, Jesusgate is hardly a new phenomenon; the early Christians, nearly two millennia closer to the source than we are, hardly knew what to make of Gospel Jesus. The orthodox trinitarian position was not hammered out until the early fourth century, and even then, it was not universally accepted. Before Christology finally gelled in the orthodox mold, there was a profusion of competing interpretations of Gospel Jesus. Origen conceded the existence of Marcion, Valentinus, Lucan, the Ophites, Cainites, Simonians, Marcellians, Harpocratians, Sibyllists, Ebionites, and Encratites.[120] Some Christian sects rejected "the doctrine of the resurrection according to scripture" and others worshipped "a god above heaven who transcends the heaven of the Jews."[121] The New Testament tells us about preachers "who do not acknowledge Jesus Christ as coming in the flesh." (2 John 1:7) No wonder poor Epiphanius needed something for headache.

The church historian Eusebius lamented the chaos of Christian belief. "Formerly [the devil] had used persecution from without as his weapon against [the church], but now that he was excluded from this, he employed wicked men and sorcerers, like baleful weapons and ministers of destruction against the soul, and conducted his campaign by other measures, plotting by every means that sorcerers and deceivers might assume the same name as our religion."[122] Accusing competing preachers of sorcery goes back to Paul—"Who has *bewitched* (*ebaskanen*) you?" (Galatians 3:1) Paul is employing "the common practice of accusing one's enemies and rivals of sorcery."[123] The *baskanos* is a sorcerer who casts spells based on malevolence and envy, a person who possesses an *ophthalmos ponēros*, an *evil eye*— "if someone preaches a gospel to you different from what you received, *a curse on him!*" (Galatians 1:9) The owner of the vineyard in Jesus' parable asks the envious workers, "Is *your eye evil (ophthalmos sou ponēros)*, because I am good?" (Matthew 20:15) The short answer to Paul's question, "Who has bewitched you?" is *other Christian preachers* who, according to Paul, engaged in *baskania*, bewitching others with the evil eye. Lest the reader be similarly bewitched by Christian preaching, a few countermeasures are humbly offered.

"The best cure for Christianity is reading the Bible."

Mark Twain

Within the ranks of modern Christians, chaos continues to reign. When they're not following the example of their forebears, hexing the competition, or talking to spirits, the Real Christians™ are usually busy defending scriptural "inerrancy," the literal truth of scripture. Because it's the basis of other doctrines peculiar to Christianity, apologists concentrate on the historical veracity of the resurrection and propose various 'minimal criteria' by which the gospel stories can be defended as real reportage. Fortunately, we can skip the thousands of pages of apologetic rhetoric and read what the gospel authors considered minimal criteria that proved a person known to be dead had returned to life. In the story of the son of the widow Jesus raised from his bier as he was being carried out for burial, a crowd saw the man come back to life and the eyewitness "were all filled with awe and praised God." (Luke 7:14-15). When Jesus raised Jairus' daughter, "Her parents were astonished." (Luke 8:56) In both cases, *onlookers personally witnessed someone known to be dead return to life*. In the case of Lazarus, the family and other mourners *personally witnessed Lazarus, who was known to be dead, exit the tomb*: "he who had died came out bound hand and foot with graveclothes." (John 11:44)

We may confidently assume the gospel writers told these stories and the early church included them in the canon of reliable, "God-breathed" books because they helped establish the belief that Jesus is "the resurrection and the life." In the gospel stories, onlookers personally witnessed someone known to be dead *come back to life* or witnessed someone known to be dead *emerge from the tomb*. But the stories of Jesus' resurrection have *no witnesses who saw Jesus come back to life and no witnesses who saw Jesus exit the tomb*. Do the gospel stories fulfill the minimum criteria established by the gospels themselves for determining when someone known to be dead has been resurrected? Conclusion: "the Bible is a self-destructing artifact...what inattentive readers call the unity of the Bible is in fact a large, and extremely fragile, cultural fiction."[124] Although believers treat gospel stories as self-validating, the most effective refutation of the New Testament remains the New Testament.

In a recently published article that examines resurrection proofs, the authors note, "In recent years, several Christian apologists (most notably, Gary R. Habermas) have claimed that a solid majority (about 75%) of scholars who have published books or articles on the subject of Jesus' resurrection accept the historicity of the empty tomb...the 75% figure is, if anything, an underestimate." Ah, but there's a catch: "a remarkably high proportion of the English-language books written about Jesus' resurrection were by members of the clergy or people linked to seminaries, which means that any so-called scholarly consensus on the subject of Jesus' resurrection is wildly inflated due to a biased sample of authors who have a professional and personal interest in the subject matter...most 'critical scholars' who study the historicity of Jesus' resurrection are not only Christians, they are also apologists, evangelists, ministers, priests, and seminary administrators or instructors."[125]

Using a similar selection of "experts," I can prove the existence of spells cast by witches, ghosts, the Illuminati, visitors from other galaxies, or any entity of my choosing. Apologists and evangelists first, and historians a distant second or not at all, Habermas and his co-religionists most resemble cryptozoologists, enthusiasts who hunt for evidence of Big Foot, the Chupacabra, and similar legendary creatures. From time to time, exciting new "evidence" of a cryptid—the Yeti, Mothman, or the Jersey Devil—appears in the literature devoted to the search. Based on purported sightings and hearsay evidence, most discoveries turn out to be pure frauds. Jesusology, like cryptozoology, has its own frauds—the James Ossuary, the Jehoash Inscription, the Shroud of Turin, and multiple forged scrolls. Although basically no one mistakes the hunt for cryptids for an academic discipline, somehow Jesusology is still considered one in some quarters.

"What can be asserted without evidence can be dismissed without evidence."

Christopher Hitchens

Hitchens' Razor—as it is commonly known—is a concise restatement of a universally acknowledged rule of discourse: the person making a claim bears the *onus probandi*, the responsibility to provide proof of the claim; it is never a skeptic's responsibility to disprove it. In short, the person making a claim is expected to supply evidence to support the claim, and if no evidence is forthcoming, the claim is dismissed. The academic custom of advancing and defending a thesis or proposition is the foundation of both debate and earning an advanced degree. The same standard of proof exists in law. An arrest must be supported by probable cause, and a crime must be proven beyond a reasonable doubt. There is no expectation that a defendant must prove himself innocent.

Hitchens directed this observation specifically at claims based on faith: "The 'evidence' for faith, then, seems to leave faith looking even weaker than it would if it stood, alone and unsupported, all by itself. What can be asserted without evidence can also be dismissed without evidence. This is even more true when the 'evidence' eventually offered is so shoddy and self-interested."[126] Despite being recognized as a fundamental epistemological principle since Aristotle, the demand that claims be supported by evidence has been the occasion of endless weeping and gnashing of teeth among apologists. As Hitchens observed, the "evidence" advanced in support of religious claims is "self-interested," based on presupposition, on *a priori* belief. It is belief in belief.

"The only way to rationally test one's culturally adopted religious faith is from the perspective of an outsider, a nonbeliever, with the same level of reasonable skepticism believers already use when examining the other religious faiths they reject."

John W. Loftus

According to legend, Romulus and Remus, the twins who founded Rome, were born of a virgin, and Perseus, we are told, was fathered on the woman Danae by Zeus. Horus and Osiris were born of virgins, as were Attis, Mithra, Adonis, and Dionysus. The birth of an important personage was announced by the appearance of a meteor or a star. Of course, no Christian in her right mind believes such rubbish for a minute, but the virgin birth of Jesus and the star of Bethlehem are real. Baby Jesus and the Star of Bethlehem are special.

Because Christianity is The One True Religion,™ the rules used to evaluate religions generally must be suspended. Christianity is the historical exception, a special case. The sturdy skepticism in force when assessing the claims of other faiths is conveniently set aside when examining the claims of Christianity. After Loftus criticized this feeble habit of special pleading by proposing the OTF, the *Outsider Test for Faith*,[127] the reaction of apologists was predictable: squealing and squawking punctuated by howling and barking. Aghast at the very notion that Christian assertions might be held to the same standards of evidence as those of

100

Islam, Hinduism, or any of scores of other creeds, the bloggers of the faith flew into an encopretic hissy fit.

As Loftus, among others notes, True Christians™ begin by presupposing the truth of the New Testament and work backward to create "evidence" for it, but as many apologists will admit about Christian claims—if pushed to the wall—"they are discerned only through the Spirit." (1 Corinthians 2:14) To others, as Paul admits, they're "foolishness." The basis of the OTF is incontrovertible: religious faith is a cultural artifact. Buddhists don't raise little Baptists. As a survey published in 2022 points out, "The parents of millennials and Generation Z did less to encourage regular participation in formal worship services and model religious behaviors in their children than had previous generations. Many childhood religious activities that were once common, such as saying grace, have become more of the exception than the norm…For as long as we have been able to measure religious commitments, childhood religious experiences have strongly influenced adult religiosity."[128]

"Religious faith is the one species of human ignorance that will not admit of even the possibility of correction."

Sam Harris

The Christian suitor arrives at history's door bearing a pungent bouquet of logical fallacies—special pleading, *tu quoque*, and question begging—but the engagement ring proffered is always the same, *presupposition*. One such suitor admits that "we *never* know the immediate context" of sayings attributed to Jesus, that Jesus "was not unique in his own time, but fits neatly into the climate of first-century Judaism," and adds, "a belief must be based on empirical evidence. What is more, the strength those beliefs are held must be in proportion to the strength and quality of the evidence that supports them." That said, the writer concludes, "The position I would advocate is confessional in nature, by which I mean one that embraces *faith-based* presuppositions [emphasis in original]...I come to the study of Jesus with certain preconceived notions, of which one is the trustworthiness of the four-fold Gospel."[129] So when push comes to shove, it's not empirical evidence but "*faith-based* presuppositions" and "preconceived notions" that determine belief, i.e., belief in belief.

Writing in a later issue of the same journal, Robert Miller critiques selective apologetic vision in action and finishes with this observation: "It is up to the evangelical camp to explain why hypothetical biographies extremely similar to the Gospels but not about Jesus should be met with sturdy skepticism, while every scholarly effort should be made to argue for the historical reliability of the canonical Gospels. Those of us in the traditional historical-Jesus camp are fairly certain that we already know why—and that reason has little (or nothing) to do with historical method and a great deal (or everything) to do with theological presuppositions. Why else would the name of the hero make such a profound difference in the historical assessment of the stories in which the hero appears?"[130] Evangelicals particularly pretend to use historical criteria to support their gospel-as-history claims and "*miraculously*, it turns out that they support the Gospel's historicity...If the application of the criteria in every case yields a positive assessment, we have not proof of historicity but doubt about the validity of the criteria."[131]

In addition to pointing out the intransigence of baseless belief and the inherent tendency to violence in religions based on scriptures,[132] Harris has identified the way such belief escapes scrutiny. "The problem with religious moderation is that it offers us no bulwark against the spread of religious extremism and religious violence. Moderates do not want to kill anyone in the name of God, but they want us to keep using the word 'God' as though we knew what we were talking about. And they don't want anything too critical to be said about people who really believe in the God of their forefathers because tolerance, above all else, is sacred. To speak plainly and truthfully about the state of our world—to say, for instance, that the Bible and the Koran both contain mountains of life-destroying gibberish—is antithetical to tolerance as moderates conceive it."[133] The moderate can never openly admit that the most extreme, the most doctrinaire, guide the whip hand of religion.

Overt violence is hardly the only threat to society posed by fundamentalism. The appearance of SARS-CoV-2 in 2019 brought with it a surge in science denialism, largely from the religious right in the US and elsewhere. It is

103

currently estimated that nearly 319,000 preventable deaths resulted in the US,[134] in large part from Jesus-Is-The-Jab idiocy vigorously propagated by the evangelical fringe. In short, preventable death from vaccine denialism in the US was the equivalent of 107 terrorist attacks on the World Trade Center.

While religious "moderates" issued pleas for sanity and compliance with basic public health measures in use since the American Revolution, religious loons continued to gather in churches despite restrictions and to spread lies and disinformation about vaccines, all the while appealing to "religious freedom." As always, the moderates were the tall grass the prayer warriors were hiding in. Religious moderates provide a façade of normality for the faith that survives on delusion, and moderate unbelievers resist speaking in blunt terms about religious insanity for fear of being perceived as intolerant.

In the United States and most of Western Europe, each generation is less likely to be religiously affiliated than the one before, and the number of unbelievers is steadily creeping upward. Rationalists would like to think this shift is due to logical argumentation being applied to belief, but I regard that as unlikely—rational argument works on the margins at best, peeling away some believers already on the verge of leaving. Instead, I suspect Christianity is mostly dying of irrelevance. The birth of Jesus is celebrated by decorating pine trees and his resurrection by hunting dyed chicken eggs—the clothes have no Emperor. Most who practice religion as adults were acculturated during childhood; as I've said several times in various venues, the best preparation for a life of delusion is a childhood spent in Sunday school. The fewer children indoctrinated, the fewer attend church as adults, and the fewer adults who attend church, the fewer children are indoctrinated.

However, another shift in belief is also underway. Internationally, Christians are moving away from traditional churches and into churches that are more openly cults. Shout-'n-holler Pentecostal sects have exploded in countries like Brazil and made substantial progress in Africa and the United States. The religious play the long game, and what begins on the fringes steadily works its way into the center. "Very often, it was the cranks who provided the conflict by which the consensus changed. They did so by working diligently on the margins until, subtly, without most of the country noticing, those margins moved...[America's] indolent tolerance of them causes the classic American crank to drift easily into the mainstream, whereupon the cranks lose all of their charm and the country loses another piece of its mind."[135] Working diligently at the margins, religious reactionaries are steadily moving world politics back to the 1950s.

If the past 2000 years of the Jesus Cult have proved anything, it has confirmed its embrace of delusion, worship of power, fetishizing of control, and its reduction of personhood to race, sex, or social position. No appeal to reason will succeed. No exhortation to the 'better angels' of human nature will suffice. Any society that hopes for sanity in its public life, for the freedom of its members, or for the ability to address crises with real solutions rather than "thoughts and prayers" will remove religion from education, from healthcare, from the judiciary, and from public policy generally.

REFERENCES

[1] One can see the various mythicist theories in my co-edited book with Robert M. Price, *Varieties of Jesus Mythicism* (Hypatia Press, 2021). For the latest view of how the Jesus character developed see Bart Willruth's two essays "Reassessing Paul's Timeline" at https://www.debunking-christianity.com/search/label/Reassessing%20Paul

[2] Lüdemann's home page: https://wwwuser.gwdg.de/~gluedem/eng/paulfounder.htm

[3] Conner, "Paul's Christianity" in Loftus, *The Case against Miracles* (Hypatia Press, 2019). For a good summary read David Madison, "The Biggest Bible Embarrassment of All?": https://www.debunking-christianity.com/2020/09/the-biggest-bible-embarrassment-of-all.html. Madison says of it, "I would say this essay is essential reading for those assembling arguments to discredit the ancient cult."

[4] Conner, "Paul's Christianity" p. 545.

[5] Carrier, "Kooks and Quacks of the Roman Empire: A Look into the World of the Gospels" at https://infidels.org/library/modern/richard-carrier-kooks/

[6] Insanity: https://dictionary.law.com/Default.aspx?selected=979

[7] Psychosis: https://www.nhs.uk/mental-health/conditions/psychosis/overview/

[8] G. A. Wells, *Cutting Jesus Down to Size: What Higher Criticism Has Achieved and Where It Leaves Christianity* (Chicago: Open Court, 2009), pp. 8-9.

[9] *ekstatsis* is the state of mind (hence the English word "ecstatsy") – one is being thrown out of his normal mind. It falls on Peter.

[10] I have defended an aphorism by Christopher Hitchens in chapter 1 titled, "In Defense of Hitchens's Razor" in *God and Horrendous Suffering* (GCRR publishing, 2021). "What can be asserted without evidence can also be dismissed without evidence." There is no relevant objective evidence for any of the miracle claims in the Bible.

[11] Michael Shermer *Why People Believe Weird Things* 2nd ed., (New York: Henry Holt and Company), 2002, pp. 283-284, and 299.

[12] "Why Bad Beliefs Don't Die" at https://skepticalinquirer.org/2000/11/why-bad-beliefs-dont-die/

[13] *Think: Why You Should Question Everything* (Prometheus Books, 2013), p. 67.

[14] See "The brain treats questions about beliefs like physical threats. Can we learn to disarm it?" at https://massivesci.com/articles/brain-political-beliefs-reaction-politics/

[15] Loftus, *The Outsider Test for Faith: How to know which Religion is True* (Prometheus Books, 2013).

[16] Stephen Law, *Believing Bullshit: How Not to Get Sucked into an Intellectual Black Hole* (Prometheus Books, 2011), p. 75.

[17] James T. Houk, *The Illusion of Certainty* (Amherst, NY: Prometheus Books, 2017), p. 16.

[18] George A. Smith, *Atheism: The Case Against God* (Prometheus Books, 1979),p. 120).

[19] Peter Boghossian, *A Manual for Creating Atheists* (Pitchstone Publishing, 2013) p. 77.

[20] Isabel Clarke, *Psychosis and Spirituality: Exploring the new frontier* (Whurr Publishers, 2001), 1.

[21] J.W. Loftus & R.M. Price (eds), *Varieties of Jesus Mythicism: Did He Even Exist?* (Hypatia Press, 2021).

[22] John G. Gager, *Kingdom and Community: The Social World of Early Christianity* (Prentice Hall, 1975), xi, 3.

[23] Gerd Lüdemann,, *Paul: The Founder of Christianity* (Prometheus Books, 2002), 240.

[24] Eldon Jay Epp, "The Multivalence of the Term "Original Text" in New Testament Textual Criticism," *Harvard Theological Review*, 92 (1999(, 245-281.

[25] Clinton Baldwin, "The Reciprocal Influence of Text and Church in the Evolution of Sacred Scripture," *History of the Church* 3 (2014), 12.

[26] Dale B. Martin, *Sex and the Single Savior: Gender and Sexuality in Biblical Interpretation* (Westminster John Know Press, 2006), 108.

[27] E.P. Sanders, *Paul: A Very Short Introduction* (Oxford University Press, 1991), 32-33.

[28] Joseph Plevnik, "The Ultimate Reality in 1 Thessalonians," *Ultimate Reality and Meaning* 12 (1989), 263-264.

[29] Lüdemann, op. cit., xxii.

[30] Paula Fredriksen, *Jesus of Nazareth, King of Jews: A Jewish Life and the Emergence of Christianity* (Vantage Books, 1999), 58.

[31] Bart D. Ehrman, *Jesus: Apocalyptic Prophet of the New Millennium* (Oxford University Press, 1999), 139.

[32] W.H.C. Frend, *The Rise of Christianity* (Fortress Press, 1984), 92-93, 97.

[33] Barry S. Crawford, "Near Expectation in the Sayings of Jesus," *Journal of Biblical Literature* 101 (1982), 226.

[34] Ibid, 227.

[35] https://www.pewresearch.org/fact-tank/2010/07/14/jesus-christs-return-to-earth/

[36] https://www.statista.com/statistics/248802/global-survey-on-the-world-ending-in-a-few-years/

[37] Joseph R. Hoffman, *Porphyry's Against the Christians: The Literary Remains* (Prometheus Books, 1994), 69-70.

[38] 1 Clement 23:3, 45:2-3.

[39] Didache 16:1, 7-8.

[40] Gager, op. cit., 21, 56.

[41] Paula Fredriksen, *From Jesus to Christ: The Origins of the New Testament Images of Jesus* (Yale University Press, 1988), 83.

[42] Didache 12:5.

[43] M. James Penton, *Apocalypse Delayed: The Story of Jehovah's Witnesses* (University of Toronto Press, 1985), 99-100.

[44] Leon Festinger, Henry W. Riecken & Stanley Schachter, *When Prophecy Fails: A Social and Psychological Study of a Modern Group that Predicted the Destruction of the World* (Martino Publishing, 2009), 3-4.

[45] Ibid, 6-8.

[46] Ibid, 28.

[47] Austin M. Harmon, *Lucian V* (Harvard University Press, 1936), 13-15.

[48] Hoffman, op. cit., 146.

[49] Wayne C. Kannaday, *Apologetic Discourse and the Scribal Tradition: The Evidence of the Influence of Apologetic Interests on the Texts of the Canonical Gospels* (Society of Biblical Literature, 2004), 144-145.

[50] Robert L. Wilkin, *The Christians as the Romans Saw Them*, 2nd ed (Yale University Press, 2003), 98.

[51] Chris Hedges, *American Fascists: The Christian Right and the War on America* (Simon & Schuster, 2008), 187-188.

[52] Hoffman, op. cit., 136-137.

[53] William O. Walker, "Postcrucifixion Appearances and Christian Origins," *Journal of Biblical Literature* 88 (1969), 157.

[54] Robert H. Stein, "Was the Tomb Really Empty?" *Journal of the Evangelical Theological Society* 20 (1977), 23.

[55] Ted Cabal, "Defending the Resurrection of Jesus: Yesterday, Today, and Forever," *The Southern Baptist Journal of Theology* 18 (2014), 116, 122.

[56] John W. Loftus, "The Resurrection of Jesus Never Took Place," *The Case Against Miracles* (Hypatia Press, 2019), 494, 496.

[57] Jeffery Lowder, *The Journal of Higher Criticism* 8 (2001), 254-255.

[58] Felicity Harley, "Crucifixion in Roman Antiquity: The State of the Field," *Journal of Early Christian Studies*, 27 (2019), 313.

[59] Geza Vermes, *Jesus the Jew* (Collins, 1973), 130-132.

[60] Philip John Hughes, "Dishonour, Degradation and Display: Crucifixion in the Roman World," *HARTS & Minds: The Journal of Humanities and Arts* 1 (2013-2014), 5, 10.

[61] Robin Lane Fox, *Pagans and Christians* (Knopf, 1987), 310.

[62] Catherine Kroeger, "The Apostle Paul and the Greco-Roman Cults of Women," *The Journal of the Evangelical Theological Society* 30 (1987), 25-26, 28.

[63] Kannaday, op. cit., 141.

[64] Ibid, 97.

[65] Gregory J. Riley, *Resurrection Reconsidered: Thomas and John in Controversy* (Fortress Press, 1994), 53.

[66] Richard Bauckham, *The Laing Lecture at London Bible College*, 2.

[67] Sider, Ronald J. "St. Paul's Understanding of the Nature and Significance of the Resurrection in 1 Corinthians XV 1-19," *Novum Testamentum* 19 (1977), 132.

[68] Idem, 124.

[69] Riley, op. cit., 53.

[70] Origen, *Contra Celsum*, VII, 35.

[71] John D. Crossan, "The Resurrection of Jesus in Its Jewish Context," *Neotestamentica* 37 (2003), 47.

[72] Robert Conner, *Apparitions of Jesus: The Resurrection as Ghost Story* (Tellectual Press, 2018).

[73] Thackeray, Henry, *Josephus: The Jewish War* (Harvard University Press, 1927), 259-260.

[74] Eusebius, *Ecclesiastical History* III, 8, 7.

[75] Martin Hengel, *The Pre-Christian Paul* (SCM Press, 1991), 54-55.

[76] David Madison, *Ten Things Christians Wish Jesus Hadn't Taught: And Other Reasons to Question His Words* (Insighting Growth Publications, 2021).

[77] Daniel F. Caner, "The Practice and Prohibition of Self-Castration in Early Christianity," *Vigiliae Christianae* 51 (1997), 397, 406.

[78] Eusebius, *Ecclesiastical History*, VI. 8.

[79] Justin Martyr, *Apology*, 29:1-2.

[8080] Frank Williams (tr), *The Panarion of Epiphanius of Salamis* (Brill, 1987), 100-101.

[81] R. Jarrett Van Tine, "Castration for the Kingdom and Avoiding the aitia of Adultery (Matthew 19:10-12)," *Journal of Biblical Literature* 137 (2018), 414-415.

[82] Patrick Connolly, "The [*doulos*] of Pauline Literature: Slavery and Freedom in the New Testament Epistles," *Concept*, Vol. XXXIX (2016), 8, 9, 11.

[83] Keith Bradley, *Slavery and Society at Rome* (Cambridge University Press, 1994).

[84] J. Albert Harrill, "Slavery and Inhumanity: Keith Bradley's Legacy on Slavery in New Testament Studies," *Biblical Interpretation* 21-4-5 (2013), 506.

[85] Catherine Nixey, *The Darkening Age: The Christian Destruction of the Classical World* (Pan Books, 2017), 176.

[86] Connally, op. cit., 3.

[87] Harrill, op. cit., 510.

[88] P.G. Kirchschlaeger, "Slavery and Early Christianity—A Reflection from a Human Rights Perspective," *Acta Theologica 2016 Suppl 23*, 68.

[89] Jennifer A. Glancy, *Slavery in Early Christianity* (Fortress Press, 2006), 156.

[90] Kimberly Flint-Hamilton, "Images of Slavery in the Early Church: Hatred Disguised as Love? *Journal of Hate Studies* 2 (2002), 27, 30.

[91] Gregory A. Boyd, *Inspired Imperfection: How the Bible's Problems Enhance Its Divine Authority* (Fortress Press, 2020), xvi-xv, 4.

[92] Kirchschlaeger, op. cit., 85.

[93] Robert J. Miller, "How New Testament Writers Helped Jesus Fulfill Prophecy," *The Case Against Miracles* (Hypatia Press, 2019), 255-277.

[94] Frank Schaeffer, *Crazy for God: How I Grew Up as One of the Elect, Helped Found the Religious Right, and Lived to Take All (Or Almost All) of It Back* (Carroll & Graf Publishers, 2007), 315, 320.

[95] Kannaday, op. cit., 35.

[96] Christopher Mount, "1 Corinthians 11:13-16: Spirit Possession and Authority in a Non-Pauline Interpolation," *Journal of Biblical Literature* 124 (2005), 316.

[97] Francis C. Thee, *Julius Africanus and the Early Christian View of Magic* (Mohr Siebeck, 1984), 382.

[98] David G. Rice & John E. Stambaugh, *Sources for the Study of Greek Religion*, corrected edition, (Society of Biblical Literature, 2009), 150.

[99] Nixey, op. cit., 147-148.

[100] Reviel Netz & William Noel, *The Archimedes Codex: How a Medieval Prayer Book Is Revealing the True Genius of Antiquity's Greatest Scientist* (Da Capo Press, 2007), 124-125.

[101] Luciano Canfora, *The Vanished Library: A Wonder of the Ancient World* (University of California Press, 1987), 192.

[102] Nixey, op. cit., 93.

[103] Samuel Brunson, "What's a church? That can depend on the eye of the beholder or paperwork filed with the IRS," *The Conversation*, February 6, 2020.

[104] Dylan Matthews, "You give religions more than $82.5 billion a year," *Washington Post*, August 22, 2013.

[105] Sarah Posner, *God's Profits: Faith, Fraud, and the Republican Crusade for Values Voters* (Polipoint Press, 2008), 172-173.

[106] Ryan Gragun, "Amid calls to #TaxTheChurches—what and how much do US religious organizations not pay the taxman?" https://theconversation.com, August 12, 2021.

[107] http://archive.boston.com/globe/spotlight/abuse/archive/extras/cover ups_archive.

[108] Bisphopaccountability.org

[109] Christina Capatides, "Catholic Church spent $10.6 million to lobby against legislation that would benefit victims of child sex abuse," www. cbsnews.com (June 6, 2019)

[110] Steve James, "Irish child abuse: The Ryan Report cover-up," www.wsws.org (26 May, 2009)

[111] "Report sheds light on Ireland's child-abuse horror,"www.benningtonbanner.com May 22, 2009)

[112] "Daingean from 1870 until 1973 in County Offaly," www.tuambabies.org

[113] Brian Kelly, "Tuam Home Survivors Network calls for exhumations bill to be thrown out," galwaydaily.com (April 15, 2021)

[114] Mindy Weisberger, "Remains of more than 1000 Indigenous children found at former residential schools in Canada," www.livescience.com (July 13, 2021)

[115] Dennis Sadowski, "Report identifies abuses of Native American children in boarding schools," *Our Sunday Visitor*, May 11, 2022.

[116] Kate Shellnutt, "Southern Baptists Refused to Act on Abuse, Despite Secret List of Pastors," <u>*Christianity Today*</u>, May 22, 2022, christianitytoday.com.

[117] Lynsey M. Barron, Esq. & William P. Eiselstein, Esq, *Report of Independent Investigation into Sexual Misconduct of Ravi Zacharias* (February 9, 2021), 4.

[118] Daniel A. Cox, "Generation Z and the Future of Faith in America," *Survey Center on American Life* (March, 2022)

[119] Frank Williams, *The* Panarion *of Epiphanius of Salamis*: Book I, 2nd ed (Brill, 2009), II, 1:2.

[120] Origen, *Contra Celsum* II, 27, III, 10, 13, V, 61-62, 64-65, VI, 19.

[121] Ibid, V, 12, VI, 19.

[122] Eusebius, *Ecclesiastical History* IV, 7.2.

[123] Jerome H. Neyrey, "Bewitched in Galatian: Paul and Cultural Anthropology," *Catholic Biblical Quarterly* 50.1 (1988), 73.

[124] Randall McCraw Helms, *The Bible Against Itself: Why the Bible Seems to Contradict Itself* (Millennium Press, 2006), 1.

[125] Michael J. Alter & Darren M. Slade, "Dataset Analysis of English Texts Written on the Topic of Jesus' Resurrection: A Statistical Critique of Minimal Facts Apologetics," *Socio-Historical Examination of Religion and Ministry*, 3.2 (2021), 368, 381.

[126] Christopher Hitches, *God Is Not Great: How Religion Poisons Everything* (Twelve Books, 2007), 150.

[127] John W. Loftus, *The Outsider Test for Faith: How to Know Which Religion Is True* (Prometheus Books, 2013).

[128] Daniel A. Cox, op. cit.

[129] Joel Willits, "Presuppositions and Procedures in the Study of the 'Historical Jesus,': Or Why I Decided Not to be a 'Historical Jesus' Scholar," *Journal for the Study of the Historical Jesus* 3 (2005), 65, 67, 69, 101, 107.

[130] Robert J. Miller, "When It's Futile to Argue about the Historical Jesus: A Response to Bock, Keener, and Webb," *Journal for the Study of the Historical Jesus* 9 (2011), 93.

[131] Amy-Jill Levine, "Christian Faith and the Study of the Historical Jesus: A Response to Bock, Keener, and Webb," *Journal for the Study of the Historical Jesus* 9 (2011), 97-98.

[132] Sam Harris, *The End of Faith: Religion, Terror, and the Future of Reason* (W.W. Norton & Company, 2004)

[133] Sam Harris, "The Virus of Religious Moderation," March 19, 2005.

[134] Brown School of Public Health, https://globalepidemics.org/vaccinations/

[135] Charles P. Pierce, *Idiot America: How Stupidity Became a Virtue in the Land of the Free* (Anchor Books, 2010), 31, 33.

Ingram Content Group UK Ltd.
Milton Keynes UK
UKHW021309050423
419696UK00021B/762

9 781087 889603